BREAKING THE ENVIRONMENTAL POLICY GRIDLOCK

The Hoover Institution
gratefully acknowledges generous support from

TAD TAUBE
TAUBE FAMILY FOUNDATION
KORET FOUNDATION

Founders of the Program on
American Institutions and Economic Performance

and Cornerstone gifts from

JOANNE AND JOHAN BLOKKER
SARAH SCAIFE FOUNDATION

BREAKING THE ENVIRONMENTAL POLICY GRIDLOCK

Edited by
TERRY L. ANDERSON

Hoover Institution Press
Stanford University
Stanford, California

Hoover Institution Press Publication No. 439

Cover photo credit: Online Image Archive

First printing, 1997
03   02   01   00   99   9   8   7   6   5   4   3

Manufactured in the United States of America
⊗ The paper used in this publication meets the minimum requirements
of American National Standard for Information Sciences—Permanence
of Paper for Printed Library Materials, ANSI Z39.48–1984.

Library of Congress Cataloging-in-Publication Data
Breaking the environmental policy gridlock / edited by
Terry L. Anderson.
        p.   cm. — (Hoover Institution Press publication : no. 439)
    ISBN 0-8179-9472-6 (alk. paper)
    1. Environmental policy—United States.   2. Environmental
management—United States.   I. Anderson, Terry Lee, 1946–
II. Series: Hoover Institution Press publication : 439.
GE180.B74   1997
363.7'056'0973—dc20   96-41981
                                                             CIP

Contents

Prologue

The 104th Congress came to Washington intent on fundamentally reforming economic, social, and environmental policies. On the economic front, the balanced budget, the line-item veto, and the flat tax at least have become ideas to be reckoned with if not actually laws on the books. Welfare reform is also on track, thanks in part to slogans such as "workfare instead of welfare" and "stop paying children to have children." Patterned after innovative programs in states such as Wisconsin, the ideas that recipients should have to work for their money, that they should be limited in the number of years they will receive welfare, and that they should be required to undergo drug testing before receiving payments are mainstream. Without a doubt, these approaches to economic and social policies have set Washington on a different and better track.

The same advances, however, have not been made with environmental policy, and in some cases ground may have been lost. Indeed, major legislation, including reauthorization of the Endangered Species Act and the Clean Water Act, has not really gotten off the ground. Congress set out to rewrite environmental laws recognizing that they were expensive to administer, fraught with litigation, and worst of all ineffective in achieving their objectives. Proponents of change argue that environmental laws punish property owners whose land harbors plants and animals and ignore the excessive costs of environmental regulations. On the heels of the spotted owl controversy, these criticisms seem to resonate with the average citizen.

Despite an overwhelming consensus that reform is necessary, little progress has been made in the environmental arena. Indeed the most significant act passed by the 104th Congress was the Senate's "salvage timber rider" that sets aside environmental laws regarding environmental impact assessment and reduces public involvement in the timber sale process. Not surprisingly this approach has come under attack from environmentalists, but it has also been questioned by average citizens who consider themselves environmentalists, if not of the extreme sort. Other proposals have called for removing federal protection of three-quarters of the areas classified as wetlands or shifting the burden of pollution cleanup from industries responsible for the pollution to taxpayers. Again these have not resonated well with the general public.

The result of this approach has been an environmental backlash against the Republican-controlled Congress. Democrats mock Republicans as the party of pollution. Vice President Al Gore challenges Republicans, saying that they "claim their environmental budget is clean and green" but that he believes "it would leave the environment black and blue." Indeed polls show that voters do not trust Republicans to take care of the environment. Even portions of the religious right have sided with the backlash by forming the Evangelical Environmental Network and noting that "God said to Noah, save all the animals."

The attacks have been effective enough to cause congressional conservatives to back away from environmental reforms, fearing that they cannot control the high ground. House Speaker Newt Gingrich is willing to take on almost any economic or social issue, but he has heeded the warnings of advisers who claim that conservatives do not have an environmental message that will play in Peoria. Advisers to congressional conservatives suggest getting the rhetoric right by talking about "preserving and protecting" but doing it "wisely and effectively." They tell members to (1) ask rhetorical questions such as "Should some Washington bureaucrat be allowed to tell you that the same water treatment regulations that apply to Alaska should also apply to Louisiana?" (2) talk about making the environment "safer, cleaner, and healthier" and about "accountability and responsibility," (3) avoid economic arguments, but if they must be used talk about "seeking a fair balance between the environment and the economy." In other words, they advise using phrases that reflect thoughtful consideration about deeply held environmental values rather than proposing substantive changes that will reduce the size of government and promote environmental quality.

But environmental policy ought to be about substance, about effective means of accomplishing environmental goals. If presented with the appropriate information, voters will agree that closing millions of acres of the federal estate to logging to save spotted owls that may not be endangered makes little sense. Spending millions of dollars to clean up Superfund sites that present little threat to humans or the environment is wasteful regardless of political persuasion. Most Americans understand that closing campgrounds in national parks in the name of budget savings when those campgrounds could be generating revenue is absurd. When the Competitive Enterprise Institute, a free market think tank in Washington, surveyed people about the Endangered Species Act, it found that only 11 percent favored the status quo; 72 percent favored reform including compensation for landowners providing endangered species habitat. Voters want substantive change. They want their environmental tax dollar spent wisely.

Without substantive reform Congress will remain gridlocked in "us against them" battles that typify Washington lobbying. Each side can claim victory in recent years. In the 1980s, environmentalists successfully blocked oil development in the Arctic National Wildlife Refuge, set aside millions of acres of wilderness, and used the Endangered Species Act to thwart development on public and private lands. When Republicans won a majority of Congress, commodity users thought it was their turn for victory. The salvage timber rider eased restrictions on logging on federal lands, and cattlemen successfully stifled grazing reform. Such us against them battles are costly and acrimonious.

But the battle lines are becoming less clear. Baby boomers are environmentalists, but they also are looking for a leaner, more effective government in Washington. Therefore producing environmental amenities for less should be an easy sell for any politician. Saving every species regardless of the costs or benefits is not acceptable to pragmatic citizens. A more acceptable approach is to put our effort into cost-effective ways of saving endangered species such as encouraging private-sector initiatives that preserve habitat.

The same principles of fiscal responsibility and individual accountability that have been applied to economic and social policies can be applied successfully to environmental policy. The choice is between positive and negative incentives, and there is ample evidence that positive incentives are more effective. Surely compensating landowners for providing wildlife habitat or leasing water from farmers for enhancing stream flows for salmon will produce more environmental amenities at a lower cost. Using positive incentives requires enforcing private property rights and encouraging voluntary exchanges as integral parts of reform. Where negative incentives are necessary to prevent polluters from violating the rights of others, clear liability rules and access to common-law remedies including compensation of harmed parties are necessary. If environmental results matter more than the means by which those results are achieved, focusing on positive incentives can get us more environmental quality for less. The key for policy reformers is to demonstrate that environmental quality can be attained more effectively with policies that emphasize positive incentives in the context of property rights and markets.

The purpose of this book is to provide that demonstration. The examples that follow do not necessarily provide a complete environmental policy agenda, but they do show policymakers and opinion leaders how we can *get the incentives right.* That is what is happening with economic and social reform, and it is what must happen with environmental reform.

Unfortunately much of the environmental rhetoric emphasizes the need for an environmental ethic without examining the important role that incentives play. This rhetoric often offers Native American culture as the quintessential example of how this ethic can work. "Conservation—Native American Style" (chapter 1) argues that ethics alone were not sufficient and that incentives were key to indigenous resource use. American Indians evolved a social order incorporating positive incentives for good resource stewardship. They husbanded land, fish, wildlife, and personal property such as horses because private ownership gave them the incentive to look toward the future. A close examination of the rich history of Native American institutions provides clues for how we might reform modern environmental policy.

Chapter 2, by Ronald N. Johnson, "Ecosystem Management and Reinventing Government," sets the stage for the environmental policy debate by illustrating how vague concepts have been used to manipulate the political process in the name of scientific management. Ecosystem management is appealing because its stated goal is "to restore and sustain the health, productivity, and biological diversity of ecosystems and the overall quality of life through a natural resource management approach that is fully integrated with social and economic goals." Professor Johnson exposes the beguiling simplicity and inherent ambiguity of this approach and explains how ecosystem management always allows the "health of the ecosystem" to trump the health of the economy rather than considering the trade-offs and interactions between the two.

In chapter 3, Terry L. Anderson and Donald R. Leal argue that the time has come for "Rekindling the Privatization Fires" for federal lands. By understanding that public lands are actually political lands, Anderson and Leal note that current federal land management is fraught with conflict and that this conflict can only be resolved by making the players face the costs and reap the benefits of their actions. Privatization is the best way of creating this nexus; short of that major strides can be achieved through contracting out, user fees, leasing, and devolution of management. According to Anderson and Leal, the growing demand for environmental amenities is stimulating the private sector to respond in innovative ways not now available on political lands. These responses should be emulated in the political sector.

Randy T. Simmons relies on evidence from his forthcoming book, *Endangered Species: Bureaucracy, Preservation, and Environment,* to argue that endangered species reform is within reach. In chapter 4, "Fixing the Endangered Species Act," he calls for transforming endangered species from liabilities into assets by compensating private landowners who provide habitat. This approach is recognized by pragmatic environmentalists as an effective way to save species. Because resource constraints will not allow us to save all species, we must find ways of saving the most important species with our limited resources. Consistent with the theme of getting the incentives rights, recognizing property rights and using markets are the avenue to meaningful endangered species reform.

Chapter 5, by Richard L. Stroup, takes us from the "romance" of natural resources to the "sludge" of the environment by considering

"Superfund: The Shortcut That Failed." Professor Stroup, one of the founders of "free market environmentalism," takes a property rights approach to the hazardous waste debate and points out that Superfund violates the "polluter pays" principle. With the Superfund legislation up for reauthorization, his proposals for solving the problem provide a framework for change that includes the polluter pays principle but requires adherence to evidentiary rules before assuming that producers are guilty of polluting. His proposals include stopping polluters when they violate the rights of others and forcing polluters to pay damages for demonstrated harm by relying on principles embedded in common law, including the requirement that the Environmental Protection Agency (EPA) meet a burden of proof when it makes accusations of harm.

In Chapter 6, Bruce Yandle suggests pragmatic reforms for air and water pollution by examining "Environmental Regulation: Lessons from the Past and Future Prospects." Like Richard Stroup, Professor Yandle outlines a property rights approach that incorporates a combination of common law, market incentives, and devolution of responsibility to lower levels of government. He shows how effluent fees have successfully reduced water pollution in Europe and how a program for trading rights to discharge pollutants into the Tar-Pamlico River basin can reduce pollution at much lower costs than the standard command-and-control approach. He calls for an environmental agenda that emphasizes goal orientation, biological envelopes, commonsense flexibility, common law, and property rights.

The proposals herein are not meant to be all-encompassing but are meant to stimulate thinking about how to break the environmental gridlock and move beyond the status quo. The emphasis is on positive incentives for both private and political decision makers. By employing positive incentives wherever appropriate, we can produce environmental amenities efficiently through voluntary exchanges. Where penalties and regulations are necessary, they should be implemented by governments closest to those problems, and they should ensure that polluters who damage others bear the cost of their actions. The market process displaces controversy with cooperation and makes the environment clean and safe.

Conservation— Native American Style

Introduction

Over the past three decades, the environmental movement has promoted a view of American Indians as the "original conservationists"—
that is, "people so intimately bound to the land that they have left no
mark upon it" (White and Cronon 1988, 417). References to this image
abound:

- "The Indians were, in truth, the pioneer ecologists of this country," said Secretary of the Interior Stewart Udall.[1]
- "I think most people in Indian country hold a set of ideals we
  should all learn from," said law professor Charles Wilkinson in a
  recent speech.[2] According to Wilkinson, these ideals teach human
  harmony with the natural environment.
- Calling for an environmental ethic patterned after that of Native
  Americans, Senator John H. Chafee recently quoted words alleg-

This chapter is based on material in Anderson (1995). Copyright © 1995, Political
Economy Research Center (PERC). Originally published in PERC Policy series.
Reprinted with permission.

edly spoken by Chief Seattle: "Man did not weave the web of life. He is merely a strand of it."

- "For many thousands of years, most of the indigenous nations on this continent practiced a philosophy of protection (first) and use (second) of the forest," says Herb Hammond in the Sierra Club book *Clearcut*. "In scientific terms, we recognize that their use of the forest was ecologically responsible—meaning that it kept all the parts."[3]

Appealing as this image of a Native American environmental ethic is, it is not accurate. The spiritual connection attributed to Native Americans frequently does not mesh with the history of Indian resource use. By focusing on the myth instead of reality, environmentalists patronize American Indians, disparaging their rich institutional heritage that encouraged resource conservation. By missing this history of Indian institutions, the environmentalists' interpretation deprives Indians and non-Indians alike of a full understanding of how we can conserve our natural heritage.

The purpose of this chapter is twofold. First, it will put to rest the myth of a unique and romantic American Indian environmental ethic. Second, it will illustrate how American Indians used complex and evolving institutions to conserve scarce natural resources and to survive in a sometimes hostile environment. By institutions, I mean the traditions, rules, laws, and habits that guided Indian societies. Although the actual laws and customs vary among societies, all societies have such institutions to guide them.

A Vision Imposed on Chief Seattle

The impression that American Indians were guided by a unique environmental ethic often can be traced to words widely attributed to Chief Seattle. "All things are connected like the blood which unites one family," Senator Chafee quotes him as saying. "Whatever befalls the earth, befalls the sons of earth."

Yet the words in the oft-quoted speech are not those of Chief Seattle;

they were written by Ted Perry, a scriptwriter. In a movie about pollution, he paraphrased a translation of the speech that had been made by William Arrowsmith (a professor of classics). Perry's version added "a good deal more, particularly modern ecological imagery," according to one historian who has researched the subject (Wilson 1992, 1457). Perry, not Chief Seattle, wrote that "every part of the Earth is sacred to my people." (Perry, by the way, has tried unsuccessfully to get the truth out.)

The speech reflects what many environmentalists want to hear, not what Chief Seattle said. The romantic image evoked by the speech obscures the fact, fully acknowledged by historians, that American Indians transformed the North American landscape. Sometimes these changes were beneficial, at other times harmful. But they were a rational response to abundance or scarcity in the context of institutions that governed resource use. Like Europeans and all people everywhere, American Indians responded to incentives.

For example, where land was abundant, it made sense to farm extensively and move on. It was common for Indians such as the Choctaw, Iroquois, and Pawnee to clear land for farming by cutting and burning forests. Once cleared, fields were farmed extensively until soil fertility was depleted; then they cleared new lands and started the process again (see White and Cronon 1988, 419–21). From New England to the Southwest, wherever Indian populations were dense and farming was intense, deforestation was common. Indeed, the mysterious departure of the Anasazi from the canyons of southeastern Utah in the thirteenth century may have been due to a depletion of wood supplies used for fuel (see Ambler 1989).

Similarly, where game was plentiful, Indians used only the choicest cuts and left the rest. When buffalo were herded over cliffs, tons of meat were left to rot or to be eaten by scavengers (see Baden, Stroup, and Thurman 1981). Samuel Hearne, a fur trader near Hudson's Bay, recorded in his journal in the 1770s that the Chippewa Indians would slaughter large numbers of caribou and musk ox, eat only a few tongues, and leave the rest to rot.

Indians also manipulated the land to improve hunting. Upland wooded areas from east to west were burned to remove the undergrowth and increase forage for deer, elk, and bison. Indeed, because of this burning, there may have been fewer old-growth forests in the Pacific

Northwest when the first Europeans arrived than there are today. In some cases, however, the improvements sought by burning were short term because these human-caused fires altered the succession of forests. In the Southeast, for example, oak and hickory forests with a high carrying capacity for deer were displaced by fire-resistant longleaf pines, which supported only limited wildlife.

Generally, the demand for meat, hides, and furs by relatively small, dispersed populations of Indians put little pressure on wildlife. But in some cases game depletion resulted from what is known as the "tragedy of the commons." This term, coined by biologist Garrett Hardin, describes what happens when no one has ownership of a resource and anyone has access to it.

Wild animals represented such a commons. They belonged to no one until they were killed. If anyone left an animal alive, in the hope that it would be there later, someone else was likely to kill it. Without ownership, no one had an incentive to protect the animals. Thus, they were overhunted, and wildlife populations fell. Anthropologist Paul Martin (1968 and 1984) believes that the extinction of the mammoth, mastodon, ground sloth, and saber-toothed cat were directly or indirectly due to "prehistoric overkill" by exceptionally competent hunters. With the advent of the Europeans, who wanted furs, Indians were able to trap furs and trade them for European goods such as beads, cloth, knives, and firearms. Where there were no institutions that limited entry into the common trapping grounds, fur-bearing populations were decimated (see Carlos and Lewis 1995). Louis S. Warren drives the final nail in the coffin of the "living in harmony with nature" myth:

> To claim that Indians lived without affecting nature is akin to saying that they lived without touching anything, that they were a people without history. Indians often manipulated their local environments, and while they usually had far less impact on their environments than European colonists would, the idea of "preserving" land in some kind of wilderness state would have struck them as impractical and absurd. More often than not, Indians profoundly shaped the ecosystems around them. (Warren 1996, 19)

Getting the Incentives Right

Although there were exceptions that led to the tragedy of the commons, generally American Indians understood the importance of getting the incentives right. Personal ethics and spiritual values were important, as they are in any society, but those ethics and values worked along with private and communal property rights. These rights strictly defined who could use resources and rewarded good stewardship.

It is sometimes difficult to fit the pre-Columbian Indian institutions into the modern context of law, government, and property rights. For example, the term *nation* is applied to Indian tribes as if the tribes were organized into formal governing structures for the entire group of Indians, similar to governments that manage modern nation-states. But most Indian tribes were made up of relatively independent groups with little centralized control except when the bands gathered for such events as ceremonies or hunts. Similarly, because Indians seldom had a written language, rules could not be codified into formal laws.

The lack of familiar modern institutions, however, by no means implies that Indians lacked rules, customary or formal. American Indian tribes were able to produce and sustain abundant wealth because they had institutions that made clear who had rights to land, fishing and hunting territories, and personal property. Pre- and post-Columbian Indian history is replete with examples of how property rights conditioned the human interface with the natural environment.

LAND AND WATER RIGHTS:
SOME COMMUNAL, SOME PRIVATE

Indian land tenure systems varied considerably, "ranging from completely or almost completely communal systems to systems hardly less individualistic than our own with its core of fee simple tenure" (Copper 1949, 1). The degree of private ownership reflected the scarcity of land and the difficulty or ease of defining and enforcing rights. Julian H. Steward (1938, 253) concludes that "truly communal property was scant" among American Indians.

Because agricultural land required investments and because boundaries could be easily marked, agricultural land was often privately owned. Unlike most private landownership today, however, Indian property was usually held by families or clans rather than individuals.

For example, families among the Mahican Indians in the Northeast possessed hereditary rights to well-defined tracts of garden land along the rivers. Recognizing this ownership, deeds of white settlers indicate that they often approached lineage leaders to purchase this land. Before European contact, other Indian tribes recognized Mahican ownership of these lands by not trespassing (Brasser 1974, 14). Away from the rivers, however, where the value of land for crops was low, it was not worth establishing ownership. As one historian put it, "no one would consider laying out a garden in the rocky hinterlands" (Brasser 1974, 7).

In the Southeast, where Indians engaged in settled agriculture, private ownership of land was common. "The Creek town is typical of the economic and social life of the populous tribes of the Southeast," writes historian Angie Debo.

> Each family gathered the produce of its own plot and placed it in its own storehouse. Each also contributed voluntarily to a public store which was kept in a large building in the field and was used under the direction of the town chief for public needs. (Debo 1970, 13–14)

Private garden plots were common in the East, as were large community fields with plots assigned to individual families. Because there were economies of scale in planting and cultivation, these tasks were done communally under the direction of a chief, but harvesting on each plot was done by the owning family, with the bounty stored in the family's own storehouse.

The Omaha tribe in what is now Nebraska cultivated private garden patches along streams. Plots were allocated on the basis of occupancy, and "as long as a tract was cultivated by a family no one molested the crops or intruded on the ground" (Fletcher and La Flesche 1992, 1:269). When the Omaha obtained the horse, as did other Plains Indians, they became more nomadic, abandoning most crop cultivation. Their tradition of private garden plots, however, carried over into the reservation era, when the tribe again allotted land to families and clans.

The Havasupai in the Southwest also considered ownership of farmland private as long as it was in use, and the Hopi Indians assigned exclusive rights to the fields to the various matrilineal clans of the village. "Each clan allotment was marked by boundary stones, set up at the corners of the fields, with symbols of the clans painted on them," wrote Kennard (1979, 554), an anthropologist. Another anthropologist notes that clan lands were marked "by numerous boundary stones . . . placed at the corners and junctions points" and "engraved on their faces with symbols of the appropriate clan" (Forde 1931, 367). The clan allotments were usually assigned to the women and became associated with a specific household through inheritance. To spread the risk associated with lack of rain or sudden flooding, each clan generally had plots in more than one location.[4]

> Dispersal of the lands of each clan over a number of sites is of very great practical importance since it reduces the risk of crop failure; where one group of fields may be washed out there remains the chance that the others may be spared. (Forde 1931, 369)

The Hopi and Zuni branches of the Pueblo Indians living in the upper Colorado basin also developed property rights reflecting their environment and production techniques. The Hopi made use of periodic flooding of their lands during the summer months by building small stone walls to check the water flow, increasing soil moisture but preventing flooding of crops. Because flood control and irrigation systems required extensive capital investment and provided economies of scale, construction was communal. Where water flowed constantly from springs on family-owned land and required little or no investment, water rights were privately owned. Florence Ellis writes:

> Technically the irrigated farmlands belonged to the Pueblo as a whole. Through assignment by the Isleta governor, an individual usually obtained a single acre of land [and the necessary water rights], but if the governor or his captains found that the assignee left the land within a year or did not farm it, the plot and accompanying water rights were returned to Pueblo possession and reassigned. (1979, 355)

Fruit and nut trees, which required long-term investment and care, were privately owned and usually inherited.[5] "So important were the piñon resources that groves of trees were considered family property in several locations" within the Great Basin area of the West, says a historian (Fowler 1986, 65). In one case a northern Paiute reflected that his father "paid a horse for a certain piñon-nut range" (Steward 1941, 440), suggesting that the property rights were valuable and tradable.

Among Indians in California, families owned piñon, mesquite, screwbean trees, and a few wild-seed patches, with ownership "being marked off by lines of rocks" (Lowie 1940, 303). Although permission to gather food was sometimes given during times of abundance, trespass was not tolerated, "the owner rebuking him [the trespasser] with such words as, 'Don't pick pine nuts here! They are not yours, but mine'" (Lowie 1940, 303). John Muir reports that the owner of a piñon tree killed a white man for felling his tree (reported in Steward 1934, 305).[6]

HUNTING: AVOIDING THE TRAGEDY OF THE COMMONS

Where Indians depended on hunting and fishing, it was imperative that they control access to general hunting territories and specific harvest sites. Without that control, the hunting grounds would be a commons that would lead to overhunting. The customary rights that governed hunting, trapping, and fishing "were often expressed in terms of religion and spirituality rather than of science as we understand it today," writes Peter Usher. "Nonetheless, the rules conserved the resource base and harmony within the band" (Usher 1992, 50). Territorial hunting rights in the north arose through use and occupancy. Often outsiders were allowed to use an area for a short period of time. Hunting groups among the Montagnais-Naskapi of Quebec between Hudson Bay and the Gulf of Saint Lawrence recognized family and clan hunting areas, particularly for beaver when it became an important trade item (Rogers and Taylor 1981, 181). Similar hunting groups and rules existed in other regions.

Quoting Indian informants, anthropologists Frank Speck and Wendell Hadlock report that for Indians in New Brunswick,

> It was . . . an established "rule that when a hunter worked a territory no other would knowingly or willfully encroach upon the region for several

generations." Some of the men held districts which had been hunted by their fathers, and presumably their grandfathers. (1946, 362)

They even had a colloquial term that translates to "my hunting ground." Frank Speck says that the Algonquian Indians from the Atlantic to the Great Lakes

> carried on their hunting in restricted, family hunting territories descending from generation to generation in the male line. It was in these family tracts that the supply of game animals was maintained by deliberate systems of rotation in hunting and gathering, and defended by the family groups as a heritage from some remote time when the country had been given to their ancestors by the Creator. (Speck 1939, 258–59)

This ownership, says Speck, led to

> the maintenance of a supply of animal and vegetable life, methods of insuring its propagation to provide sources of life for posterity, the permanent family residence within well-known and oftentimes blazed property boundaries, and resentment against trespass by the family groups surrounding them who possessed districts of their own. (1939, 259)

Indian tribes of western North America defended their hunting, fishing, and gathering territories against trespass (see Steward 1938, 254). Steward reports that among Paiute Indians of the Owens Valley in California, "communal groups stayed within their district territory" (Steward 1934, 252), which was bounded by natural features such as mountains, ridges, and streams. Each distinct Apache band, says Keith Basso,

> had its own hunting grounds and, except when pressed by starvation, was reluctant to encroach upon those of a neighbor. . . . Each local group had exclusive rights to certain farm sites and hunting localities, and each was headed by a chief who directed collective enterprises. (1970, 5)

Customs and norms regulated the harvest. There was a district headman who determined where and when to hunt based on his knowledge from the past.

FISHING: WELL-DEFINED RIGHTS

In the Pacific Northwest, Indians had well-defined fishing rights.[7] To capture salmon returning from the ocean to spawn in freshwater streams, Indians placed fish wheels, weirs, and other fixed appliances at falls or shoals where the fish were naturally channeled (Netboy 1958, 11).

Their efficient technology could have depleted salmon stocks, but they realized the importance of allowing some of the spawning fish to escape upstream. Robert Higgs (1982, 59) quotes a Quileute Indian born about 1852:

> When the Indians had obtained enough fish they would remove the weirs from the river in order that the fish they did not need could go upstream and lay their eggs so that there would be a supply of fish for future years.

In an important case regarding Indian fishing rights in the Northwest, Judge George Boldt noted that "individual Indians had primary use rights in the territory where they resided and permissive use rights in the natal territory (if this was different) or in territories where they had consanguineal kin."[8] In many cases the fishing sites were inherited by sons from their fathers (Higgs 1982, 59).

Relying on salmon as their main source of food, the coastal Tlingit and Haida Indians established clear rights to fishing locations where salmon congregated on their journey to spawning beds. Access to these locations was limited to the clan or house group. In addition to property rights to the salmon streams, these Indians had rights to "bear- and goat-hunting areas, berry and root patches, hot springs, sea otter grounds, seal and seal lion rocks, shellfish beds, cedar stands and trade routes" (Langdon 1989, 306).

The management units could exclude other clans or houses from their fishing territories. When territories were infringed on, the trespasser was required to indemnify the owning group or face potentially violent consequences (see Oberg 1973 and De Laguna 1972).[9] Management decisions were generally made by the *yitsati*, the "keeper of the house," who had the power to make and enforce decisions regarding harvest levels, escapement, fishing seasons, and harvest methods. This eldest clan male possessed superior knowledge about salmon runs, escapement, and fishing technology and was therefore in the best position to be the "custodian or trustee of the hunting and fishing territories" (De Laguna 1972, 464). Although there is debate over just how powerful the *yitsati* was (see Olson 1967), it is clear that salmon runs were sustained over long periods by rules made locally.

Unfortunately, the white man's law usurped these secure Indian fishing rights and replaced them with a system that encouraged the tragedy of the commons. It was "economically inferior to the property system originally established by the tribes," one scholar concludes (Barsh 1977, 23).

PERSONAL ITEMS: PRIVATE

Although ownership of land and natural resources varied considerably, personal items were nearly always privately owned. Clothes, weapons, utensils, and housing were often owned by women, for whom they provided a way to accumulate personal wealth. For the Plains Indians, the tepee offers an example. Women collected enough hides (usually between eight and twenty), tanned and scraped them, and prepared a great feast where the hides were sewn together by the participants.

The effort required to produce items of personal use ensured that they became private property. Weeks or months could be spent collecting buffalo hides for tepees. Time was spent chipping arrowheads, constructing bows and arrows, and weaving baskets. One historian illustrates the point:

> Water, seed, and hunting areas, minerals and salt deposits, etc., were freely utilized by anyone. But once work had been done upon the products of natural resources (mixed labor with them) they became the property of the person or family doing the work. Willow groves could be used by anyone, but baskets made of willows belonged to their makers. Wild seeds could be gathered by anyone, but once harvested, they belonged strictly to the family doing the task. (Steward 1934, 253)

In other cases, the raw materials themselves were scarce, and these, too, were private property. Stone from which arrowheads were chipped was personal property obtained through long-distance trade. Special wood for bows was traded; for this to happen the wood had to be privately owned. In short, property rights reflected the degree of scarcity of the good.

Consider trader Charles Larpenteur's description, written in 1860, of a wealthy Blackfoot man: "It is a fine sight to see one of those big men among the Blackfeet, who has two or three lodges, five or six wives, twenty or thirty children, and fifty to a hundred horses; for his trade amounts to upward of $2,000 a year" (1898, 401). Converting this amount to 1990 dollars, such a man had an annual income of approximately $500,000!

Perhaps the best example of private ownership was the horse, which was acquired by Plains Indians in the latter half of the eighteenth century. The horse revolutionized transportation and hunting. A good horse could be ridden into a stampeding buffalo herd so that arrows could be shot at close range. By following the buffalo, the Plains Indians could live a life of abundance.

The horse became one of the Indian's most important sources of wealth. "A buffalo runner of known ability was worth several common riding horses or pack animals" (Ewers 1958, 78). In Canada in the early 1800s, a buffalo horse could not be purchased with ten guns—a price far greater than any other tribal possession (Barsness 1985, 61).

Given their value, horses were well-cared for and closely guarded. "No system of branding was used, but each person knew the individualities of his horses so that he could recognize them," writes Clark Wissler (1910, 97). Apparently disputes over ownership were few, but if a horse was stolen, the offense was punishable by death. Perhaps more than any other asset, the horse reflects the extent to which Indian culture utilized the institution of private ownership.

Additional Positive Incentives

The above discussion makes clear that property rights were an integral part of Indian culture and that they encouraged resource conservation. But even where activities were communal, positive incentives, including incentives similar to ownership, made success possible.

Rabbit hunts among Indians of the Great Basin were conducted communally. These hunts required leadership and nets into which the rabbits were driven; those nets were privately owned and maintained (Freed 1960, 351). To provide a positive incentive for the communal hunt, the leader of the hunt and the owners of the nets received a bigger portion of the catch (Fowler 1986, 82).

On a buffalo hunt, the successful hunter was "entitled to keep the skin and some choice portion of the meat for his family" (Steward 1938, 253). An elaborate nomenclature was used by the Omaha to describe rewards for those who killed and butchered buffalo. "To the man who killed the animal belonged the hide and one portion of *tezhu'* [side of meat] and the brains." Other portions were as follows: "To the first helper to arrive, one of the *tezhu'* and a hind-quarter; to the second comer, the *u'gaxetha* [includes the stomach, beef tallow, and intestines]; to the third, the *tethi'ti* [ribs]" (Fletcher and La Flesche 1992, 1:273).

The hunters marked their arrows distinctively, so that, after the hunt, the arrows in the dead buffalo would indicate which hunters had been successful (Ewers 1969, 160). Disputes over whose arrow killed the buffalo were settled by the hunt leader. Poorer families followed the hunt and depended on the charity of the hunters for meat (Ewers 1969, 162).

It took strong, well-disciplined horses to run into a stampeding herd and keep up with the buffalo. Four or five buffalo cows might be killed "on a single chase by the best Blackfoot marksman with the best horse under him. Most hunters rarely killed more than one or two buffalo at a chase. Men with inferior buffalo horses had to be satisfied with killing the slower running bulls" (Ewers 1969, 159).

If an owner decided to loan his horse for a chase, payment was expected. Three Calf described to John Ewers (1969, 161) the arrangement his father made when loaning his horse. "There was no agreement in advance for any payment to be made to my father. If the man was selfish and offered my father no meat, the next time he wished to borrow horse, father told him, 'No.'" The chase was dangerous and a loaned horse might be injured. Generally, the responsible borrower who had taken reasonable precautions to prevent injury did not have to pay damages, but the irresponsible borrower was forced to replace the lost horse.

In sum, faced with the reality of scarcity, American Indians understood the importance of incentives and built their societies around institutions that encouraged good human and natural resource stewardship. In particular, clearly specified property rights helped encourage conservation of scarce resources. Ethics and spiritual values may have inculcated a respect for nature, but an elaborate set of social institutions that today would be considered private property rights punished irresponsible behavior and rewarded stewardship. As Louis Warren (1996, 22) puts it,

> Among other things, Indian history is a tale of constant innovation and change. . . . If there is a single, characteristic Indian experience of the environment, perhaps it is the ability to change lifeways in radical fashion to maintain culture and identity.

Wildlife Management: Lessons Lost and Lessons Learned

Today, there are abundant natural resources throughout Indian country. These resources would be better managed if tribes would return to their rich heritage of positive rewards for good stewardship instead of relying on romantic and sometimes mythical worldviews promoted by non-Indian environmentalists.

Wildlife management on Indian reservations offers a distinct contrast between lessons lost and lessons learned from the history of Indian culture and institutions. In many respects, Indians on reservations have tremendous assets. They have asserted sovereign claims to fish and wildlife, both on and off reservations. Relying on treaties signed in the nineteenth century, courts have granted Indians rights to large resources. Indians have rights to half the harvestable salmon and steelhead in the Pacific Northwest. They may use gill nets not available to non-Indian fishers in the Great Lakes. They may hunt walrus and polar bears without regulation by the state of Alaska. In Wisconsin, they have special hunting privileges on public lands, including an eighty-five-day deer season, and permission to hunt from vehicles.

Unfortunately, wildlife managers on most reservations have lost sight of the value of institutions like those described earlier in this chapter. After asserting their claims, they have often created a wildlife commons, and the consequences have been devastating. Case after case illustrates the decimation of wildlife populations (see Williams 1986, 59–64).

- Indian gillnetting for salmon on the West Coast has wiped out major runs of salmon on the Klamath/Trinity River system.

- Waste is pervasive. The Alaska Fish and Game Department documented one case of 214 caribou carcasses left to rot and "counted 24 caribou left whole—there was a snow machine track to each one. . . . Most had been there a considerable time" (quoted in Williams 1986, 73).

- On most western reservations, big game species are often almost nonexistent. On the Crow Reservation in Montana, for example, there are few big game animals such as deer and elk, despite the fact that the reservation has excellent habitat. According to a tribal wildlife official, non-Indians are not allowed to hunt on the reservation but tribal members can hunt year around without limits. The few big game animals that may be found wander in from outside; they are not managed on a sustainable basis.

One writer describes what can happen when wildife belongs to everyone:

Over the past 25 years Shoshones and Arapahos, equipped with snowmobiles, AFV's and high-powered rifles, have virtually wiped out elk, deer, moose and bighorns on the 2.2 million-acre Wind River Reservation in Wyoming. Repeated motions for modest self-regulation emanating from within the reservation have been defeated by vote of the tribal leaders. . . . in one confined area 31 dead elk were found. In another, a retired Indian game warden mowed down an entire herd of 14. Meat piled up at local dumps. Antlers were exported to the Orient where antlers and horns are ground to a powder and hawked as an aphrodisiac. (Williams 1986, 63)

Lessons Learned: The White Mountain Apache

Fortunately, one wildlife success story in Indian country illustrates the power of incentives. This is the story of the White Mountain Apache of east-central Arizona. The members of this tribe are managing their trophy elk population and other wildlife opportunities on a sustainable basis—and making a profit.[10]

The Fort Apache Reservation covers 1.6 million acres with a diversity of habitat from oak chaparral at lower elevations to mixed coniferous forests at higher elevations. This habitat supports about twelve thousand free-ranging elk. To get some idea of the success elk hunters enjoy, consider the reservation's track record. From 1977 to 1995, nontribal hunters have taken ninety bull elk that were recorded in either Boone and Crockett or Safari Club record books. (In comparison, this is about the number of record elk that have been taken from the entire state of Montana since record keeping began in 1932.)

Since 1980, hunters on guided trophy elk hunts have enjoyed a 90 to 95 percent success rate. The average score for antlers has been 366 Boone and Crockett points (comparable to a foursome averaging three under par for a round of golf). Yes, the resource base is large, the habitat is prime, and, according to reservation biologists, the genetics of the herd are ideal for producing trophy elk. But entrepreneurship played a pivotal role in Fort Apache.

Before 1977, elk hunting on the reservation provided good hunting compared with nearby national forest lands, but it was nowhere near the quality of hunting that exists today. At that time, the state of Arizona issued seven hundred nontribal elk permits at $150 each for hunting on the reservation. The state permits were required in addition to a tribal license, but the tribe received none of the revenues collected by the state. Each license entitled the bearer to shoot a bull elk regardless of size. Typical of state agencies, this policy maximized the number of hunter opportunities rather than the value of the hunt.

Fortunately for both the tribe and the elk, tribal leaders decided that they could capitalize on the market for trophy elk. In 1977, tribal chairman Ronnie Lupe, with the backing of the eleven-member tribal council, informed the state that the tribe would allow elk hunting without a state permit and would control all hunting and fishing on the reservation. The state opposed this but acquiesced after a federal court decision. The tribe's first order of business was to reduce the hunting pressure on immature bull elk by ending the general elk hunt and replacing it with a trophy elk hunt. Permits to hunt elk were reduced from seven hundred to thirty, and the price per permit rose from $150 to $1,500. Revenues from the sale of these reservation permits went to the tribe's general fund.

The trophy elk hunting program blossomed. Mature bulls as a percentage of all bulls increased to 73 percent, and the number of record book elk taken rose from three in the final six years of state management to eight per season. In addition to promoting trophy elk production, the tribe also designed a quality hunting experience, free from the crowded conditions on public lands.

The tribe tapped into a mother lode of hunter demand. In 1995, revenues from trophy elk hunting exceeded $850,000. Sixty-six hunters paid $12,000 each for a seven-day trophy hunt. A special auction for four additional openings was also held, with an average winning bid of $24,000 and a high bid of $30,000. Despite the $12,000 price tag, there is a five-year waiting list of hunters willing to pay.

Less-expensive hunting opportunities also exist that offer a way to maintain the proper bull-to-cow ratio in the herd and help manage other wildlife species. For example, the tribe periodically issues one hundred antlerless permits priced at $300 each, which have a hunter success rate of 80 percent. The tribe also offers hunting permits for bear ($150), javelina ($75), and wild turkey ($750). It costs $50 a season or $5 a day to hunt quail, squirrel, and cottontail rabbit.

In addition to hunting, the tribe manages other resources for amenity values and collects fees. Although most reservation lakes and streams are open to bait fishing, certain select waters are restricted to flies and lures. Fish species include native Apache, brown, brook, and rainbow trout and some arctic grayling. Yearly fishing permits are priced at $80, summer permits at $50, and day permits at $5. There is even a rent-a-lake program, which allows Cyclone and Hurricane Lakes in their entirety to be rented for $300 a day, with a three-day minimum. Fishing has proved lucrative, generating $600,000 in revenue in 1995. When revenues from services such as camping, boating, and river rafting are added, amenity-based recreation enterprises generated nearly $2 million in 1995. These enterprises compare well with the tribe's logging operation, casino, and ski resort as sources of revenues and jobs. Entrepreneurship and management institutions that conserve wildlife have benefited the White Mountain Apache Reservation and the wildlife on its territory.

Back to the Future through Better Institutions

American Indian history teaches us that we must go beyond calls for spiritual awakenings and find workable institutions that provide positive incentives for good stewardship. Because American Indians adapted their institutions to the resource constraints, they were able to sustain life, often in hostile environments. Property rights were an integral part of American Indians' heritage. Refocusing on these institutions, as the White Mountain Apache have done, offers the best way for Native American cultures to manage their resources on a sustainable basis.

Non-Indians also will do well to stop promulgating myths as a solution to modern environmental problems. Especially in a multicultural society where worldviews vary widely, devolution of authority and responsibility offers the best hope for resource conservation. Rather than shunning property rights solutions, we should embrace them, as did our predecessors on this continent.

Notes

1. Quoted in Williams (1986, 30).

2. Wallace Stegner lecture at Montana State University reported in the *Bozeman Daily Chronicle*, April 19, 1996, p. 9.

3. Hammond quoted in Devall (1993, 182).

4. For an extensive discussion of "Hopi Agriculture and Land Ownership," see Forde (1931).

5. See Kennard (1979, 554–57) and Forde (1931) for details.

6. For a more complete discussion of property rights to piñon trees, see Lowie (1940).

7. For a more complete discussion, see Higgs (1982).

8. *United States v. Washington* (1974), 384 F. Supp. 312, 352–53.

9. Consistent with economic theory (see Demsetz 1967 and Anderson and Hill 1975), the Tlingit did not establish territorial claims to streams where species such as the pink or dog salmon were abundant (Olson 1967, 12). They also treated the open ocean as a commons because their technology did not allow overexploitation of salmon in this environment. Some bands, however, did claim ownership of bottom fishing grounds for halibut and cod.

10. Information about the White Mountain Apache program comes from tribal officials.

References

Ambler, J. Richard. 1989. *The Anasazi*. Flagstaff: Museum of Northern Arizona.

Anderson, Terry L. 1995. *Sovereign Nations or Reservations? An Economic History of American Indians*. San Francisco, Calif.: Pacific Research Institute for Public Policy.

Anderson, Terry L., and P. J. Hill. 1975. "The Evolution of Property Rights: A Study of the American West." *Journal of Law and Economics* 18(1): 163–79.

Baden, John, Richard Stroup, and Walter A. Thurman. 1981. "Myths, Admonitions, and Rationality: The American Indian as a Resource Manager." *Economic Inquiry* 19(1): 132–43.

Barsh, Russell L. 1977. *The Washington Fishing Rights Controversy: An Economic Critique*. Seattle: University of Washington Graduate School of Business Administration.

Barsness, Larry. 1985. *Heads, Hides, and Horns*. Fort Worth: Texas Christian University Press.

Basso, Keith H. 1970. *The Cibecue Apache*. New York: Holt, Rinehart and Winston.

Brasser, Ted J. 1974. "Riding on the Frontier's Crest: Mahican Indian Culture and Culture Change." Paper no. 13, Ottawa, National Museums of Canada, Ethnology Division.

Carlos, Anne M., and Frank D. Lewis. 1995. "Strategic Pricing in the Fur Trade: The Hudson's Bay Company, 1700–1763." In *Wildlife in the Marketplace*, ed. Terry L. Anderson and Peter J. Hill. Lanham, Md.: Rowman and Littlefield Publishers.

Copper, John M. 1949. "Indian Land Tenure Systems." In *Indians of the United States*, contributions by members of the Delegation, and by advisers to the Policy Board of the National Indian Institute, for the Second Inter-American Conference on Indian Life, Cuzco, Peru.

Debo, Angie. 1970. *A History of the Indians of the United States*. Norman: University of Oklahoma Press.

De Laguna, Frederica. 1972. *Under Mount Saint Elias: The History and Culture of the Yakutat Tlingit*. Smithsonian Contributions to Anthropology. Vol. 7 (in 3 parts). Washington, D.C.: Smithsonian Institution Press.

Demsetz, Harold. 1967. "Toward a Theory of Property Rights." *American Economic Review* 57(2): 347–59.

Devall, Bill. 1993. *Clearcut: The Tragedy of Industrial Forestry.* San Francisco, Calif.: Sierra Club Books and Earth Island Press.

Ellis, Florence Hawley. 1979. "Isleta Pueble." In *Handbook of North American Indians.* Vol. 9. Washington, D.C.: Smithsonian Institution, 351–65.

Ewers, John C. 1958. *The Blackfeet: Raiders on the Northwestern Plains.* Norman: University of Oklahoma Press.

———. 1969. *The Horse in Blackfoot Indian Culture.* Washington, D.C.: Smithsonian Institution Press.

Fletcher, Alice C., and Francis La Flesche. 1992. *The Omaha Tribe.* 2 vols. Lincoln: University of Nebraska Press.

Forde, C. Daryll. 1931. "Hopi Agriculture and Land Ownership." *Journal of the Royal Anthropological Institute of Great Britain and Ireland* 61: 357–405.

Fowler, Catherine S. 1986. *Handbook of North American Indians—Great Basin.* Vol. 11. Washington, D.C.: Smithsonian Institution.

Freed, Stanley A. 1960. "Changing Washo Kinship." *Anthropological Records* 14(6): 349–418.

Higgs, Robert. 1982. "Legally Induced Technical Regress in the Washington Salmon Fishery." *Research in Economic History* 7: 55–86.

Kennard, Edward A. 1979. "Hopi Economy and Subsistence." In *Handbook of North American Indians.* Vol. 9. Washington, D.C.: Smithsonian Institution.

Langdon, Steve. 1989. "From Communal Property to Common Property to Limited Entry: Historical Ironies in the Management of Southeast Alaska Salmon." In *A Sea of Small Boats,* ed. John Cordell. Cambridge, Mass.: Cultural Survival.

Larpenteur, Charles. 1898. *Forty Years a Fur Trader on the Upper Missouri: The Personal Narrative of Charles Larpenteur,* ed. Elliott Coues. Vol. 2. New York: F. P. Harper.

Lowie, Robert H. 1940. "Ethnographic Notes on the Washo." *American Archaeology and Ethnology* 36: 301–51.

Martin, Paul S. 1968. "Prehistoric Overkill." In *Pleistocene Extinctions: The Search for a Cause,* ed. Paul S. Martin and Herbert E. Wright Jr. New Haven, Conn.: Yale University Press.

———. 1984. "Prehistoric Overkill: The Global Model." In *Quaternary Extinctions,* ed. Paul S. Martin and Richard G. Klein. Tucson: University of Arizona Press.

Netboy, Anthony. 1958. *Salmon of the Pacific Northwest: Fish vs. Dams.* Portland, Oreg.: Binfords and Mort.

Oberg, K. 1973. *The Social Economy of the Tlingit Indians.* American Ethnological Society Monograph 55. Seattle: University of Washington Press.

Olson, R. L. 1967. "Social Structure and Social Life of the Tlingit in Alaska." *Anthropological Records* 26.

Rogers, Edward S., and J. Garth Taylor. 1981. "Northern Ojibwa." In *Handbook of North American Indians—Subarctic.* Vol. 6. Washington, D.C.: Smithsonian Institution.

Speck, Frank G. 1939. "Aboriginal Conservators." *Bird Lore* 40: 258–61.

Speck, Frank G., and Wendell S. Hadlock. 1946. "A Report on Tribal Boundaries and Hunting Areas of the Malecite Indians of New Brunswick." *American Anthropologist* 48(3): 355–74.

Steward, Julian H. 1934. "Ethnography of the Owens Valley Paiute." *American Archaeology and Ethnology* 33(1): 233–324.

———. 1938. *Basin-Plateau Aboriginal Sociopolitical Groups.* Smithsonian Institution, Bureau of American Ethnology, Bulletin 120. Washington, D.C.: U.S. Government Printing Office.

———. 1941. "Cultural Element Distributions: XIII Nevada Shoshoni." *Anthropological Records* 4(2): 209–59.

Usher, Peter J. 1992. "Property as the Basis of Inuit Hunting Rights." In *Property Rights and Indian Economies,* ed. Terry L. Anderson. Lanham, Md.: Rowman and Littlefield Publishers.

Warren, Louis S. 1996. "Seeing the People for the Trees: The Promise and Pitfalls of Indian Environmental History." *OAH Magazine of History* (spring): 18–23.

White, Richard, and William Cronon. 1988. "Ecological Change and Indian-White Relations." In *History of Indian-White Relations,* ed. Wilcomb E. Washburn. Vol. 4. Washington, D.C.: Smithsonian Institution.

Williams, Ted. 1986. *Don't Blame the Indians: Native Americans and the Mechanized Destruction of Fish and Wildlife.* South Hamilton, Mass.: GSJ Press.

Wilson, Paul S. 1992. "What Chief Seattle Said." *Environmental Law* 22: 1451–68.

Wissler, Clark. 1910. "Material Culture of the Blackfoot Indians." *Anthropological Papers of the American Museum of Natural History* 5(1): 1–176.

Ecosystem Management and Reinventing Government

Although most of the public has never heard the term *ecosystem management*, its usage is widespread among environmental groups, and it is gradually becoming the management philosophy of federal and state agencies in charge of land and aquatic resources.[1] The ideas underlying ecosystem management are not new, but recent events have brought about a sense of urgency and calls for changes in resource management practices. At the Forest Conference held in Portland, Oregon, in April 1993, President Clinton declared that "for too long, contradictory policies from feuding agencies have blocked progress, creating uncertainty, confusion, controversy, and pain throughout the region" (quoted in Gore 1993, 52). Similarly, Secretary of the Interior Bruce Babbitt has frequently used the phrase "economic-environmental train wrecks" to describe clashes between economic objectives and environmental laws.[2] These conflicts have contributed to the current administration's efforts to examine how federal agencies conduct their business and propose changes. According to the language of Vice President Al Gore's National Performance Review, federal agencies are to be reinvented so that they will work better and cost less. Ecosystem management is to be an integral part of this reinvention (Gore 1993).

Definitions and interpretations of ecosystem management abound, as do perceptions on whether and how it will work. But make no mistake about it, ecosystem management is not simply a new name for old resource management practices such as multiple use. Indeed, the debate over ecosystem management is about whose values will determine resource management practices in both the public and the private sectors.

At first blush, the basic notion behind ecosystem management is compelling. An ecosystem is an interconnected and complex community of living things, including humans. Therefore, understanding how alterations to one part of an ecosystem can cause changes throughout is clearly essential to the successful management of these systems. To adequately sustain the diversity and productivity of ecosystems requires a comprehensive management approach, one that avoids the historical focus on the protection of single species and recognizes that legal and political boundaries may have little or no relation to the scale appropriate for a ecosystem. In practice, ecosystems can be large, encompassing numerous private owners and political jurisdictions. Accordingly, ecosystem management is about working across administrative and political boundaries to manage for ecological integrity. Importantly, ecosystem management is to be a collaborative approach that integrates ecological, economic, and social factors. It involves the forming of partnerships between federal, state, and local government, Indian tribes, landowners, and other stakeholders.

The above description of ecosystem management is essentially the same as the one promoted by the White House–organized Interagency Ecosystem Management Task Force (hereafter, Task Force). But exactly what are the goals of ecosystem management? Although preferring the term *ecosystem approach*, the Task Force (1995, 3) specified the following objective for ecosystem management:

> The goal of the ecosystem approach is to restore and sustain the health, productivity, and biological diversity of ecosystems and overall quality of life through a natural resource management approach that is fully integrated with social and economic goals. This is essential to maintain the air we breathe, the water we drink, the food we eat, and to sustain natural resources for future populations.

This statement seems to have something in it for everybody, which is undoubtedly its purpose. But, as argued in this chapter, there is more in it for some groups than for others. The emphasis on the need to restore and sustain ecosystems reflects an acceptance of the view that the ability of the world's resource base to nourish future generations adequately is in serious jeopardy. One motivating assumption for ecosystem management is that rising world populations have gravely deteriorated the earth's resources. It promotes the idea that the environmental health of the nation is seriously threatened and that a new approach to resource management is required. Although the ecosystem management approach recognizes that the economic well-being of the populace is a worthwhile consideration, that objective can supposedly be achieved only by maintaining healthy ecosystems. The underlying message is that there is a positive relationship between healthy ecosystems and the economy. Taking care of ecosystems takes care of the economy—truly a win-win outcome.

The practice of examining complex systems and interactions is familiar to economists. Given the relatively broad view of ecosystems espoused under ecosystem management, economics would seemingly be an integral part of that approach. Economists, however, tend to view healthy ecosystems as one desirable goal among many, often insisting on putting comparable values on hard-to-measure factors such as biodiversity. But because a healthy ecosystem is the goal of ecosystem management, little time is spent considering the benefits and costs of various actions such as protecting biodiversity. Trade-offs between preservation and logging, grazing, and mining on federal lands will continue to be made, but the criteria delineating for whom and on what basis these trade-offs will occur are not identified in the Task Force report or in any of the government's ecosystem management documents.

The purpose of this chapter is to critically examine the Task Force report, the underlying motivation for ecosystem management, and the implementation problems posed by this approach. Although ecosystem management is supposedly based on the "best science" (Task Force 1995, 3), much of the justification offered for this approach lacks scientific support.[3] As explained in this chapter, ecosystem management is predicated on an unjustifiable fear of ecological collapse and misunderstandings about the way economies operate. Moreover, ecosystem management, with its emphasis on a collaborative approach and healthy ecosystems, is vague, making it unclear how trade-offs are to be managed and how the performance of those ultimately responsible for critical management decisions will be judged. As a consequence, ecosystem management will not bolster the Clinton administration's efforts to reinvent the federal bureaucracy.[4]

There are, however, positive aspects to ecosystem management. The emphasis on collaboration has brought some disparate groups to the table. Achieving a better understanding of other parties' stakes in the ecosystem management process appears to have reduced conflict and encouraged a more open dialogue, one objective of ecosystem management. As discussed in the concluding remarks, there is a growing sense that the recent heavy-handed, top-down regulatory approach to resource management has had perverse effects. Although this recognition is encouraging, ecosystem management has a high price tag attached to it.

The Pretense of Knowledge, Calamity, and the Evolution of Ecosystem Management

Aldo Leopold (1949), author of the renowned *Sand County Almanac* and Wilderness Society cofounder, was one of the earlier proponents of the ecosystem approach. His metaphors suggest the interconnection among parts: People should take care of the land as a "whole organism," paying attention to see that the "cogs and wheels" were in good working order. If people did these things, the land would remain productive. Leopold knew well that people were and were going to remain an integral part of ecosystems, but he also shared the philosophies of John Muir, who preached that it was essential to preserve the unity and harmony of nature. The preservationist approach, however, went well beyond maintaining the productivity of the soil for growing crops. Spearheading this movement was a righteous infatuation with primitive wilderness and the notion that these areas could be maintained intact and even restored if nature were left alone by man to do its handiwork.

The preservationist's view, however, had limited appeal in the 1950s. Although some land practices were considered harmful, the green revolution was under way and the potential to improve crop yields seemed unlimited. The idea that some lands should be set aside as parks and that some human uses should be restricted had its supporters. But the prevailing opinion was that land and water resources were to be scientifically managed for the production of commodities (Dana and Fairfax 1980). With the exception of the national parks, federal land managers emphasized forest growth and timber harvests, and grazing was an integral part of most systems. Fire and floods were to be controlled, and wildlife was to be managed to maintain or increase populations of game species.

Early in the 1960s, however, questions about the earth's capacity to sustain production and its resiliency to shocks were being raised. Rachel Carson (1962) warned us about the disastrous effects of DDT on wildlife, and the environmental movement began to pick up speed.[5] Attendance at the first Earth Day rallies on April 22, 1970, revealed to politicians that the environmental movement had achieved a critical mass that could no longer be ignored. Federal land management policies, and certainly the practices of large private landowners, did not sit well with those who believed that man had already tampered enough with the unity and harmony of nature. The cutting of old-growth timber was especially offensive. The ancient forests of the West Coast were disappearing. The fact that a stand of timber cut today starts taking on characteristics of an old-growth forest within eighty to a hundred years provided little consolation to those who sought to preserve it.[6] Nor would it satisfy preservationist desires to point out that nature is dynamic and ever changing, a principle of evolutionary ecology since Darwin (Chase 1995). Instead, preservationists argued that, in the absence of human disturbance, ecosystems were purposeful and self-regulating.

Proponents of preservation found support and initial credibility in a new field called cybernetics. Developed by mathematicians during the Second World War for application to weapons systems, cybernetics is concerned with the design of automatic control devices. At the heart of cybernetics are feedback loops, wherein energy flows operate to keep systems stable in the face of disturbances. By utilizing the principles of cybernetics, it could be argued that ecosystems were self-regulating, capable of maintaining themselves in equilibrium.[7] Moreover, communities with a highly diversified mix of organisms were better able to persist and ward off natural disturbances than communities with fewer, less-diversified organisms. The argument was complete: preservation made sense because it was natural, and biodiversity was important because of the role it played in keeping natural systems in balance.

In the early 1970s, this new theory of ecology advanced another step up the policy ladder. Barry Commoner (1971) argued that everything is connected to everything else and that ecosystems need to be protected from outside forces that can intervene and disturb their natural equilibrium. He also stressed that were the inherent stability of these systems allowed to be destroyed by man's actions, the result could be total ecological collapse. Of course, nothing could be more threatening to mankind. The only way to avoid this pending catastrophe was for humans to drastically alter their lifestyles. Because synthetics had a particularly negative impact on the environment, extensive regulation of their use was necessary. This meant restricting the use of fertilizers, detergents, and petroleum products. Biological diversity had to be protected by isolating threatened habitats from human interference. Anything less meant that the sustainability of civilization itself would be in jeopardy.

Environmentalists could no longer be dismissed as merely advocating the preservation of nature to protect amenities. They were attempting to protect the human race from itself. The environmental impacts already generated from technological advances following the end of the Second World War were sufficient to threaten the continued development of the world economic system. If the human species were to survive, many of these technological advances would have to be redone to bring the world's productive technology into harmony with the demands of its ecosystems.

Although this argument may have been new to some, the notion that humans threaten their own survival by their exploitation of nature is a theme that predates the Industrial Revolution. Concern with the long-term supply of natural resources dates back to the writings of Malthus at the end of the sixteenth century. A fixed land base and growing population meant a dismal future for the human species. Nevertheless, both world population and per capita income have risen substantially since the time of Malthus.

Those who held the belief that a state of calamity was nearly upon us were not dissuaded by the failures of Malthus's prediction or by the results of studies undertaken in the 1950s and 1960s that examined resource scarcity. The best known of these studies was Barnett and Morse's

Scarcity and Growth (1963). Examining data for the period 1870 to 1957 and using a variety of measures of resource scarcity, Barnett and Morse found little cause for alarm. In general, the relative prices of natural resources had not risen over time as predicted by the Malthusian model. Barnett and Morse attributed this outcome to three general factors: (1) the substitution of more-plentiful lower-grade resources for less-abundant high-grade resources; (2) the discovery of new mineral deposits; and (3) technological advances in both the extraction process and the use of resources as inputs.

The findings of Barnett and Morse did not deter environmentalists who believed that current rates of resource use were unsustainable.[8] After all, if changes were not made the continuous degradation of matter and energy would, according to the law of entropy, mean disorder. Environmentalists interpreted that law to mean that there was little time left to make the necessary corrections (Daly 1977).

The belief that disorder was imminent was encouraged by results obtained from large computer models of the world economy that incorporated natural resource constraints. Similar in spirit to the new ecology models that employ cybernetics, these growth models contained feedback loops that allowed for interactions between population growth, production, resource use, and pollution. The best known of these models is the one constructed by Meadows et al. (1972) for the Club of Rome's project on the predicament of humankind. The system was calibrated to track key variables from 1900 to 1970, and forecasts were then made to the year 2100. The results indicated that, without swift and radical changes in the way humans interact with the environment, the future was dismal. Population and pollution would increase over time, and eventually the system would collapse. In one of the main simulation runs, food per capita and industrial output begin to fall shortly after the year 2000. To avoid disaster, population had to be stabilized by setting the birthrate and death rate equal in 1975, and industrial capital, which pollutes the world and makes ecosystems less productive, was to be stabilized by setting net investment equal to zero by 1990. Even then, there was no guarantee that ecosystem collapse, and thus collapse of the world economy, could be avoided. The underlying message was that here was a scientifically based picture of the future, one that incorporated feedback loops and derived from high-speed computers. Although the draconian measures recommended in the Club of Rome report were not undertaken, growth in per capita food consumption and the output of goods and services worldwide show no sign of leveling off.[9]

The predictive power of the Meadows model was seriously flawed because of its underlying assumptions. The model contained a set of interrelated dynamic equations, but the system is not nearly as complex and encompassing as its authors would have us believe. Essentially, these modelers assumed a linear growth rate for all good things and an exponential rate for bad things. Inevitably, trouble cannot be too far away. Completely absent from the model was the basic economic concept that prices influence behavior. As resources are depleted, rising prices induce conservation and the development of substitutes. If the possibilities for resource discovery, recycling, and substitution in production are included, obviously the collision between population growth and resource scarcity is delayed. With minor changes in the underlying parameters of the model, collapse could be avoided even if population growth continued to expand until the year 2100 (Cole et al. 1973). Nevertheless, models like that of Meadows created an atmosphere of fear that, absent drastic change, collapse is imminent.

To avoid this collapse, ecologists began to argue that preserving biodiversity by protecting ecosystems was essential. Their message was instrumental in the passage of and later support for the Endangered Species Act of 1973 (ESA) (16 U.S.C. sec. 1531–44). Although preserving biodiversity by protecting ecosystems was the objective environmentalists sought with passage of the ESA, the act included penalties for taking endangered species. The architects of the act took the individual species approach because they thought there was no true objective means for measuring diversity, suggesting that the concept of biodiversity is not operational.[10] Operationalism is important because it implies a correspondence between abstract concepts of a scientific theory and the experimental operation of physical measurement (Bridgman 1936). If the concept of biodiversity is not operational, it is legitimate to question whether claims about its importance to the world's economies can ever be tested empirically. If it cannot be tested, it would fail the conventional criterion that distinguishes science from nonscience (Popper 1965).

The lack of an operationally scientific concept is evident in the ESA. Plaintiffs under the act need only show only that a human action had or would have a negative impact on an endangered species; they do not need to nor can they show that the relevant ecosystem is also imperiled. For the proponents of the act, this is unnecessary because endangered species are indicators of ecosystem health; they are the "canaries in the mine."

But how important is any particular species to the stability of an ecosystem? Ecosystems typically contain hundreds to thousands of interacting species. The emerging consensus, however, is that only a small number of these species are the "drivers" while the others are "passengers" (Heywood 1995, 833). Basically, only a small set of biotic and physical processes is critical in forming the structure and overall behavior of an ecosystem. Even these distinctions may not be meaningful because the deletion of one set of species may allow alternative species to take over a particular function with little underlying change in the functioning of the ecosystem. Although the deletion of some key species may trigger a transformation from one type of ecosystem to another, knowledge of which species are the drivers and how the system will react is generally lacking. In short, the scientific basis for the ESA is absent.

This lack of scientific basis, however, has not slowed the application of the ESA. As of April 30, 1996, a total of 959 species were listed as threatened or endangered under the act.[11] But, despite the public funds devoted to protecting these species, as well as the high costs imposed on private landowners and users of the public lands, species continue to decline and become extinct. Indeed, only about five have been removed from the list because of successful recovery (Mann and Plummer 1995, 239–47). Although habitat degradation by humans has clearly contributed to this decline, ecosystems are not permanent fixtures. Evolutionary change was taking place long before humans discovered the chain saw. To suggest, however, that humans allow some species such as the northern spotted owl to go extinct—an unlikely event in the near term even without protection because its population is far greater than originally thought (Chase 1995, 365)—invites an emotional response. Persons suggesting such a course demonstrate that they are willing to risk the collapse of an ecosystem. After all, famed Harvard biologist E. O. Wilson (1988) argues that it is reckless to suppose biodiversity can be diminished indefinitely without threatening humanity itself. The statement surely is correct, but just where are the boundaries? Are no trade-offs to be allowed?

This approach to protecting biodiversity is similar to the President's Council on Sustainable Development's extensive use of the "precautionary principle." Under this principle, society is to take reasonable actions to avert risks to human health and the environment even in the face of scientific uncertainty. Instead, however, this policy has fostered the pursuit of almost perfect safety and has been costly relative to the benefits obtained (Viscusi 1993; Van Houtven and Cropper 1996). Most arguments for protecting ecosystems and biodiversity, however, are not predicated on conventional benefit-cost analyses.

Along with demands to protect biodiversity has been a growing call for the reframing of environmental values. Humans are to reinterpret their place on the planet as one species among many. Because everything is dependent on everything else, all living things are of equal worth. This radical approach, referred to as biocentrism, requires that ecosystem health take precedence over the wants and interests of humans.[12] Biocentrism is also evident in the ecosystem management approach.

In a widely cited article, Edward Grumbine (1994) synthesized a variety of views on ecosystem management. He explains that it is an evolving concept, where the focus is on systems, not on individual species. It is a process that requires working across administrative and political boundaries, emphasizes the use of science, and promotes adaptive management. Certainly, focusing on systems rather than on individual species makes sense. But the following set of ecosystem management goals, which Grumbine (1994, 31) claims are most frequently endorsed, reveals that this approach is not about minor alterations to the status quo. Those goals are to

- Maintain viable populations of all native species in situ
- Represent, within protected areas, all native ecosystem types across their natural range of variation
- Maintain evolutionary and ecological processes
- Manage over periods of time long enough to maintain the evolutionary potential of species and ecosystems

- Accommodate human use and occupancy within these constraints

Although there are to be protected areas, this supposedly is not a pure preservationist approach because it is both ecological and evolutionary processes that are to be maintained. Contradictorily, "all" native species and ecosystem types are also to be maintained. Unlike native species, however, exotic species, regardless of their use value to humans, are not worth maintaining. The fifth item in the list is most telling. Although humans may be a part of an ecosystem, they are merely to be "accommodated." As Grumbine (1994, 31) notes, "These fundamental goals provide a striking contrast to the goals of traditional resource management." Indeed, they suggest a whole new world order, a means for redefining the way economies operate. Although some of the wording used by Grumbine differs from that endorsed by the White House–organized Task Force, there are also unmistakable similarities.

Ecosystem Management at the Federal Level: The Task Force Report

The justification given by the Task Force for implementing ecosystem management is similar to the long-standing alarmist concerns addressed above. The challenge is that population growth is reaching the limits of our natural resources. According to the Task Force (1995, 4), population growth makes it essential that we change the way humans interact with ecosystems because "human history is replete with examples of communities and civilizations that have fallen with the loss of a natural resource base." The example given to support this claim is the Hohokam people of Arizona, who were forced to abandon their lands half a millennium ago because they irrigated incorrectly. No doubt there are more examples like this, and these ancient mistakes, if such they were, mean that "unbridled competition and conflict over natural resources must give way to cooperation, sharing, and maintaining reasonable and sustained uses of natural resources." Following this prescription, we can move from extraction to reclamation and environmental protection.

The Task Force frequently refers to the blight of ecosystems, but there is no reference to the fact that a number of measures of environmental quality have improved over time. For example, data from the U.S. Environmental Protection Agency (1994) indicate that concentrations of many air pollutants have exhibited a downward trend since 1975. In addition, forest acreage in many parts of the country has expanded since the 1950s, and the long-term outlook for the world's timber supply is positive (Sedjo and Lyon 1990). Ignoring these improvements, which took place in the absence of ecosystem management, the Task Force (1995, 17) proclaims that "the ecosystem approach integrates ecological protection and restoration with human needs to strengthen the essential connection between economic prosperity and environmental well being." There is, of course, a connection, but the Task Force (1995, 23) promotes the idea that the direction of causation is from the environment to the economy.

> Natural resource conflicts have been assumed to pit environmental concerns against economic development. We now recognize that it is wrong to think in terms of "either/or," that is, framing issues around the false choice of either environmental protection or economic development. Long-term economic prosperity depends on sustaining ecosystem functions.

The Task Force (1995, 24) offers southern Florida and the greater Yellowstone ecosystem as examples. The Florida Everglades is upheld as "a pillar of southern Florida's economy," and the "true wealth" of the Yellowstone region is in its natural amenities that offer a desirable lifestyle, not in its extractive industries like logging and mining. These conclusions ignore the fact that cities such as Las Vegas are among the fastest-growing areas in the country.[13] Just because some people have a strong desire to live in areas abundant in natural and ecological resources, it does not follow that expenditures on restoration and preservation are justified. For example, slowing growth and spending billions of federal and local tax dollars to restore the Florida Everglades, as the Clinton administration has proposed, is not likely to enhance the economy of southern Florida.[14] Supporters of ecosystem management appear to be under the delusion that natural environments are like the ball field in the movie *Field of Dreams*—restore them and economic growth will follow. The desire by proponents to link ecosystem management and ecosystem health to a prosperous economy is understandable. Failure to do so would likely mean voter rejection of costly restoration projects. Reliance on the false premise that supply creates its own demand is potentially costly if causation goes in the opposite direction.[15]

Despite frequent mention of concern for healthy economies, there is little indication that those promoting ecosystem management have given the subject much thought. Consider the Task Force's (1995, 5) comments on the economic impact of listing the northern spotted owl: Although "some communities are still struggling, . . . what was billed as an agonizing choice of jobs versus owls has proved not to be a dilemma at all." No economic analysis of the impact of the northern spotted owl on the economies of the Pacific Northwest is presented. Instead, the Task Force (1995, 6) offers the reader a quote from the mayor of Springfield, Oregon, who claims that "owls versus jobs was just plain false. What we've got here is quality of life. And as long as we don't screw that up, we'll always be able to attract people and business." Supposedly, the reduction in timber harvests has so improved the quality of life in the Pacific Northwest that business has flocked there to set up shop.

Indeed, if one simply focuses on the overall performance of the economies of the states of Oregon and Washington, the massive reductions in public timber harvests in those states do not appear to have had much effect.[16] Population growth rates have exceeded the national average, and growth in personal per capita income has been somewhat greater in Oregon and Washington than for the country as a whole.[17]

But the economies of these states, of course, are influenced by sectors other than the timber industry. Sales of Boeing aircraft, Windows 95, and shipments to and from Pacific Rim countries, to name a few, are important factors in the health of these economies. Indeed, less than 4 percent of total employment in Oregon and Washington is attributable to the forest products industry. The reduction in timber industry employment by approximately twenty-five thousand jobs (U.S. Forest Service 1992), or about one-fifth of industry employment, clearly had local impacts that in some cases were especially harsh (Chase 1995). But these reductions were not great enough to significantly lower long-term aggregate employment, especially when compared with a large employment base. People are resilient and tend to be mobile. Although the immediate impact of job loss can be high, most individuals find other alternatives. Thus simply focusing on what has happened to aggregate employment obscures the overall cost and the distribution of cost resulting from preservation.[18]

The opportunity cost of not cutting trees, referred to as stumpage value, can be enormous.[19] If the timber harvest is restricted to protect the spotted owl, society sacrifices the lumber and other wood products obtainable from those stands. In addition, restricting harvesting means that the value of plant and equipment that are specialized to the timber industry is also lost.

Importantly, the decision to save a species is not an all-or-nothing choice but a marginal one. Hence, the appropriate question becomes how much should be sacrificed to increase the likelihood that the spotted owl will not go extinct? Montgomery, Brown, and Adams (1994) estimate that increasing the likelihood of owl survival to 82 percent, a goal comparable with the recovery plan proposed by the Department of the Interior in 1992, would cost $21 billion.[20] The Interagency Scientific Committee's conservation proposal, which would affect both public and private lands, could increase the probability of survival to 95 percent, but total costs would increase to $46 billion. Whether the benefits of preservation, including the full range of ecological services, are worth these costs has not been measured. But merely suggesting, as the Task Force did, that jobs in the Pacific Northwest have not decreased as a consequence of restrictions on harvesting ignores the true costs of preservation.

If ecosystem management is truly concerned with the operation of global ecosystems with humans as an integral part, it must take into account the possibility that economic growth positively affects the environment. Consider the general proposition that environmental quality is a good that people eventually demand more of as their incomes rise. Initially, economic growth may cause environmental degradation, but after some point further increases in income lead to a relative shift in the types of goods people prefer, with one of those goods being the quality of the environment. Essentially, poor people attempt to satisfy their basic material well-being first, deferring amenities until their incomes have risen. This inverted U-shaped hypothesis has been tested empirically by examining whether high-income countries do more to maintain and clean up their environments than do poorer countries (e.g., Selden and Song [1994]; Grossman and Kreuger [1995]). The inverted U-shaped curve appears to hold for a number of important pollutants, including the level of sulfur dioxide, carbon monoxide, nitrogen dioxide, and suspended particulate emissions, as well as poor sanitation and impure water supplies.[21] Granted, these results do not mean the earth's resource base is capable of supporting indefinite economic growth (Arrow et al. 1995). But the results do suggest that carelessly promoting costly restoration programs and overly stringent restrictions on human uses of the ecosystems could cause both economic well-being and the health of ecosystems to decline.

Sustainability is another important concept promoted under the banner of ecosystem management. The concept of sustainability has been a hallmark of policy debates on resource use for decades. Despite the emphasis it has received, definitions of sustainability are vague. Nonetheless, it is a popular notion that today's population should not squander the earth's resources to the detriment of future generations. Recognizing that it is physically impossible for one generation to leave the world's natural resources in the same condition in which it found it, the simple fact is that future generations have generally done better than past generations. Worse yet, trying to leave future generations with the same resource endowment might actually make them poorer because resource use enables the production of durable goods, such as bridges, works of art, and, importantly, knowledge. These become part of the wealth one generation passes on to the next.

Although sustainability is generally considered in a global context, the Task Force focuses on the sustainability of local communities within ecosystems. Given wide fluctuations and trends in world prices, however, the sustainability of resource-dependent local communities is beyond their control. And where the community's output is large relative to the world market, restricting timber harvests to protect some local endangered species can raise world prices and increase harvesting activities elsewhere. This may have an even more negative impact on fragile ecosystems and communities less able to cope with change (Sedjo 1995). Although ecosystem management is supposedly a comprehensive approach, there is little in the Task Force's report to suggest how conflicts like those between local objectives and global consequences are to be resolved. Other than reliance on collaborative efforts, guidelines for weighing conflicting objectives are either vague or absent.

Implementing Ecosystem Management: The Problem Areas

One objective the Task Force (1995, 19) set for federal agencies was the development of common principles to guide them in implementing the ecosystem approach. Although this concept is new to some agencies, others adopted elements of this approach years ago. In 1968, for example, the Park Service endorsed the policy of ecosystem management for the nation's parks (Chase 1995, 113). The policy stressed the concept of preservation of entire systems as compared with the protection of individual species. It assumed, however, that parks were whole ecosystems, an assumption that caused considerable difficulties. In the case of grizzly bear management, biologists Frank and John Craighead concluded that the bears' needs could not be met solely within the borders of Yellowstone Park (Craighead 1979). It was becoming apparent to the proponents of ecosystem management that politically determined borders were artificial lines with little correspondence to the boundaries of ecosystems.

Failed attempts to manage within these artificial boundaries became the impetus for the current, more expansive, ecosystem management approach. A much-utilized aerial photograph in discussions of ecosystem management supposedly reveals the foolishness of politically or administratively determined boundaries. The photo is of the western boundary between Yellowstone National Park and Targhee National Forest. On the national park side, timber expands to the distant horizon, whereas on the national forest side, there are large cutover areas right up to the boundary. The message is that "barriers impede the implementation of ecosystem management" (U.S. General Accounting Office 1994, 55). Unfortunately, ecosystem management provides no guidelines for determining ecosystem boundaries (Fitzsimmons 1994). Indeed, in practice ecosystems can range "from a garden plot to a forest to the entire planet"

(Keiter 1994, 301). Ecosystems are vague concepts, and, as such, they pose special problems for federal agencies and their constituents.

Considering the situation illustrated in the above-mentioned photo, does ecosystem management mean that timber is to be harvested from the national park while harvests are reduced on adjoining national forests? Or that naturally started fires are to be allowed to burn both within the park and within the national forest? This is a case of two federal agencies that historically have had very different constituencies (Dana and Fairfax 1980). At least since 1960, the guiding principle of the Forest Service has been multiple-use and sustained-yield management. Although recreational use has been an expanding component of the Forest Service mission, that agency is still largely concerned with commodity uses such as timber, grazing, and mining. In contrast, the Park Service is mainly driven by preservationist concerns and recreational demands. The Task Force (1995, 32) acknowledges that "federal agencies are driven by their authorizing legislation. Most existing federal statutes were not written with interagency coordination in mind." Given the disparities in their missions, just what set of common principles are these agencies to develop that will guide them in implementing the ecosystem approach?

Benefit-cost analysis seemingly would be a candidate to satisfy the Task Force's request for a common set of principles that would guide decision making. After all, if done correctly, benefit-cost analysis would incorporate social, economic, and ecological factors.[22] One advantage of using benefit-cost analysis is that it would compel federal resource managers to consider the trade-offs involved when making decisions and to make those trade-offs public. As such, benefit-cost analysis offers a method for judging whether ecosystem management is merely a special-interest group approach to resource use or an approach that attempts to account for the diverse and conflicting demands placed on ecosystems. Although federal agencies like the Forest Service are already required to consider project benefits and costs in their planning activities, it has not evolved as the guiding management principle for those agencies.[23] Under ecosystem management, the role of benefit-cost analysis will be downplayed even more. Indeed, the Task Force does not mention the use of benefit-cost analysis. Instead, it emphasizes setting "ecological goals" and knowing the "threshold levels of human-induced stress" (Task Force 1995, 50).

It is not at all clear what the pursuit of ecological goals is supposed to mean in terms of each agency's mission. Nor is it clear what is meant by the mandate to maintain healthy ecosystems. The fact that ecosystem management is such a vague concept poses special problems for the Clinton administration's efforts at reinventing government.

In response to concerns about the ability of government to deliver goods and services to voters, the Clinton administration has launched a major effort to bring private-sector business concepts into the bureaucracy.[24] Vice President Al Gore's (1993) National Performance Review committee initiated an effort to reform the federal bureaucracy by adopting total quality management, employee empowerment, and other business management tools. Under total quality management, bureaucratic personnel rigidities are to be removed. Central to this approach is a change in the incentive system within organizations to provide flexibility and motives for improving performance. But this objective requires clear job descriptions, definite performance goals, objective performance appraisals, and a reward structure that emphasizes merit-based promotion and compensation.[25] Accordingly, adoption of a vague managerial objective like ecosystem management is likely to diminish any hope of installing meaningful private-sector performance incentives into the federal civil service.

Indeed, because the concept of ecosystem management is so vague, adoption will likely lead to even greater problems of accountability and performance.[26] The problem with the current civil service system is that it lacks strong incentives for employees to perform, while at the same time providing career employees with the opportunity for considerable discretionary behavior that allows them to promote their own personal objectives or beliefs.[27] This condition raises questions about the control that the president and Congress have over an increasingly professional bureaucracy.[28]

Professionalism has expanded rapidly in the federal government during the post–World War II period. As government services have become more complex, there has been greater reliance on professional training, certification of federal employees, and scientific management.[29] Working for professional objectives with which one agrees would seem to be especially important in an environment where financial incentives for performance are largely absent. Further, professional and career links with outside groups can offer incentives to government employees to resist the implementation of policies that are incompatible with their own career objectives. In situations where government employees hold strong personal preferences, the notion that they will be neutral civil servants is naive.[30]

At federal agencies in charge of environmental and natural resources, the shift toward a more professional bureaucracy has been accompanied by changes in the professional composition of these agencies. An example of the effects of changing political conditions and apparent independent behavior on the part of agency personnel, sheltered by civil service rules, is provided by the U.S. Forest Service. Herbert Kaufman (1960) once described Forest Service personnel as highly motivated and dedicated to the agency's main mission. Throughout much of its history, the Forest Service's mission centered on providing services and commodities to the timber and grazing industry. In the 1960s and 1970s, the professional staff of the agency was composed largely of people trained in timber management and harvesting, foresters and engineers who supervised timber sales and road construction to access sites. The political success of the environmental movement greatly changed the mission of the agency and pitted interest groups against one another. These conflicts resulted in a change in the types of professionals employed by the Forest Service. Individuals trained in wildlife management, biologists, and specialists in recreation became more common. For example, in 1972 there were 4,945 professional foresters and only 121 wildlife biologists in the Department of Agriculture, almost all employed by the Forest Service. In comparison, the number of foresters in 1991 was 5,399, while the number of wildlife biologists had expanded to 1,159.[31]

With the change in professional orientation within the Forest Service, there has been a growth in the number of employees who actively challenge agency policy. These individuals want the Forest Service to move more completely toward environmental goals, such as wilderness preservation, and away from past policies in support of the timber industry. Agency employees with professional ties to new policies and strongly held beliefs about their implementation have latitude within the civil service system to act as advocates. For instance, the Association of Forest Service Employees for Environmental Ethics, with a claimed membership of two thousand, openly encourages employee opposition to timber sales.[32] In the private sector, such actions would likely bring dismissal. Although career federal employees can be, and occasionally are, dismissed, civil service rules offer them greater protection than is available to private-sector employees.

When organizations cannot provide workers with clear objectives, employees are more likely to engage in the gaming or distortion of policy. These circumstances seem to fit the federal government's approach to ecosystem management. Although the Task Force repeatedly mentions the need to build consensus and resolve conflict, it also recognizes that resource users and private landowners remain suspicious of the objectives of ecosystem management. The Task Force (1995, 25), however, labels these reactions as "misunderstandings about the ecosystem approach." The Task Force could have better used its time attempting to understand why there is so much distrust of federal natural resource and environmental policy, rather than attempting to place a new label on old and failed ideas about the relationship between ecosystems and the world economy.

Concluding Remarks

Ecosystem management is advertised as a "common sense way for public and private managers to carry out their mandates with greater efficiency" (Task Force 1995, 3). This new approach is also a means for building consensus. But what incentive do private landowners have to come to the table? Maintaining ecosystems and biodiversity may well be an objective landowners endeavor to promote simply because they believe it is important for their own lives and for society in general. Moreover, recognition that one's actions have a negative impact on other people and the resource base can influence people's behavior. The behavior of firms and individuals is governed, in part, by the cultural environment in which they operate. Some environmental ethos, although lacking formal legal sanctions, can have influence, and this ethos can bring private landowners to the table. But they will also come because failure to participate will be costly.

Commodity users of the federal lands have little choice. They must participate or the process will proceed without them. Ecosystem management can be like a town hall meeting. If you fail to show up, it is an indication that you are not interested, not a true stakeholder. There is, however, another more compelling reason for the private sector to participate in ecosystem management—the Endangered Species Act (ESA). Although ecosystem management is supposedly nonconfrontational and collaborative, there is a "hammer" in the background and that hammer is the ESA. This act has been a key force in bringing ecosystem management into the national policy arena. To avoid the "train wrecks" of the past, steps must be taken to accommodate economic development before crises evolve. For example, under the ESA's Habitat Conservation Plan, the secretary of the interior can enter into agreements with private landowners that permit "incidental takes" of listed species if landowners agree to long-term conservation programs to protect ecosystems. Landowners who obtain approval will not be subject to later demands from the federal government for larger land set-asides or financial commitments even if the needs of species change over time. Ecosystem management offers a "no surprises" policy and the possibility of "one-stop shopping for multiple-permit requirements by agencies that coordinate their actions on an ecosystem basis" (Task Force 1995, 22). By participating in dialogues on ecosystem planning, developers can help shape the permitting process, albeit to the disadvantage of their competitors. Although their own development costs may rise, the costs incurred by their rivals can go up even more. These are incentives that entrepreneurial developers find hard to resist. In addition, the timber industry, beleaguered by a constant barrage of claims that it is misusing the earth's resources, has accepted the promise that ecosystem management will provide a balanced forum.

Indeed, a potential benefit of ecosystem management is that, by fostering dialogues among disparate groups, cooperation and trust can be established, helping to heal the social wounds caused by the last thirty years of conflict over environmental issues. There is evidence that this process is beneficial. A research project conducted by the School of Natural Resources and Environment at the University of Michigan examined seventy-seven ecosystem management projects around the country (Frentz et al. 1995). Many of those projects involve grassroots coalitions of private landowners and nonprofit organizations such as the Nature Conservancy who then work closely with federal and state agencies to help restore and maintain natural processes. There is also a general consensus evolving that government-driven, top-down approaches to problem solving are not working (Keystone Center 1996).

In place of the heavy emphasis on regulations, market-based incentives need to play a more dominant role than they have in the past. Economic incentives that reduce the difference between the value of wild resources to private individuals and their value to society as a whole should be used in place of regulations. That will require the development of effective institutions that force users of the natural environment to take account of all costs and benefits. Many of the examples offered by Anderson and Leal (1991), such as establishing property rights to instream flows, could help in the process of maintaining and restoring ecosystems. And Stroup's (1995, 9) suggestions on how to turn listed "species from an enemy to friend" could result in many more species being unlisted than has been accomplished under the current failed program of the U.S. Fish and Wildlife Service.

Although there are positive aspects to ecosystem management, it should be remembered that many of its supporters promote the idea that the world is facing environmental calamity and that drastic actions are required. To them, ecosystem management means substantially less harvesting of timber, no clear-cutting, bans on the use of chemicals, strict controls on population growth, and a whole new world economic order. These draconian policy measures have been argued for in the past, with claims that they were needed to avoid imminent disaster. The underlying premise of ecosystem management is essentially this same failed message. Despite the proclamation that the best science must be used, it is religiously held beliefs that drive this approach. Ecosystem management comes with a lot of heavy baggage that must be jettisoned if the true objective is to ensure that humans derive the highest net benefits from the world's ecosystems. This will require that those attempting to implement this approach obtain a greater understanding of how economies operate and of the importance of market incentives and property rights in providing and protecting environmental resources.

Notes

1. If the reader doubts that the term *ecosystem management* is receiving widespread usage, a check of the Internet will prove informative. The author's search using Webcrawler uncovered 58,697 documents containing the phrase *ecosystem management.*

2. See Fitzsimmons's (1994) discussion about the use of the phrase *train wrecks* and whether ecosystems can be defined in a consistent manner.

3. It is striking the number of times descriptions of ecosystem management mention that this new approach emphasizes the use of "the best science." Thus ecosystem management is scientific management. But this nation has been down this failed path before. See Nelson (1995).

4. Besides performance, the other major problem with the federal bureaucracy is a lack of accountability. Accountability has to do with the latitude available to administrative agencies for engaging in opportunistic behavior of their own in the implementation of congressional statutes and the administration of policy (McCubbins, Noll, and Weingast 1989). Agency officials are in a position to channel programs and services to favored constituents, to expand agency mandates and budgets, and to act on their personal preferences in ways that deviate from the desires of Congress and the president (Johnson and Libecap 1994). As argued in this in chapter, rather than being a solution to the problems of accountability, the ecosystem management approach will likely lead to a heightening of these problems.

5. Although Carson's book was highly influential, thirty years after its publication the evidence that DDT is dangerous to wildlife, in a comprehensive sense, is still being debated. See, for example, Avery (1995).

6. There is no precise definition of old growth. Although regenerated Douglas fir forests of the Pacific Northwest begin to take on many of the characteristics of a climax forest after 80 to 100 years, the classification scheme utilized by the U.S. Forest Service will normally require that stands be 200 to 250 years old before classifying them as old growth. By that criterion, there are approximately 10.3 million acres of old-growth forests in California, Oregon, and Washington. See Bolsinger and Waddell (1993).

7. One of the classic early articles on this subject was by Hutchinson (1948). Also see Hutchinson (1978). It should be noted that theories of economic growth often utilize dynamic equations with functional forms similar to those used by

population ecologists. Notions of equilibrium growth paths and steady-state solutions are also a standard part of these neoclassical growth models, which actually predate the models of population ecologists. However, these models have performed poorly when used to explain why some countries have experienced substantial economic growth and others have languished. For a discussion, see Olson (1996).

8. As pointed out by Brown and Field (1978), there are some potential problems with Barnett and Morse's measures of resource scarcity. For example, if property rights to the resource are not well defined, prices may not reveal growing resource scarcity. Although the process of defining property rights to ocean fisheries is still in its infancy, most of the other commodities examined by Barnett and Morse had fairly well-defined rights by the late nineteenth century.

9. Although data on total production are clearly not precise, Food and Agricultural Organization of the United Nations (various years) statistics for the last ten years indicate that per capita production has been increasing.

10. See Chase (1995, 109). All concepts of diversity imply some measure of distance between species (Weitzman 1992), but there is no agreement on which method provides the "best" measure of diversity.

11. In addition, the U.S. Fish and Wildlife Service lists 564 foreign species as endangered or threatened. Importation of these species is restricted. Source, U.S. Fish and Wildlife Service, Internet information service, http://www.fws.gov/.

12. This view is well expressed by Thomas Stanley (1995, 261), who argues that "humanity must begin to view itself as part of nature rather than the master of nature. It must reject the belief that nature is ours to use and control."

13. In recent years, Las Vegas has been the fastest-growing large metropolitan area in the country. Between 1990 and 1994, growth was 26.2 percent. The second fastest, at 20.2 percent, was the McAllen-Edinburg-Mission metropolitan statistical area in Texas (U.S. Department of Commerce 1995).

14. The goal of the South Florida restoration project (South Florida Water Management District 1995, 10) is to return the Everglades ecosystem "to conditions that approximate, to the maximum degree practical, pre-impact conditions." The motivating factor for this restoration project is to encourage the recovery of fifty-six listed species. The project involves the restoration of natural flows to the Everglades. The capital cost for the project is approximately two billion dollars, with 35 percent of that total to be provided by the federal government and the remainder to come from state and private sources. The annual operating budget is projected to be approximately 240 million dollars (source, South Florida Ecosystem Restoration, FY 1996 Budget Cross-Cut). Because this project involves a multitude of federal, state, and local governments, as well as Indian tribes and private landowners, it is an excellent example of the ecosystem management approach. It should be mentioned, however, that the project does

not have final approval, and there is much opposition to it from landowners, not to mention the local taxpayers who have yet to see the full bill.

15. Despite early promises, the creation of Redwood National Park did not generate sufficient tourist visits to offset a substantial decline in the logging sector. As a consequence, the local economy declined. See Chase (1995, 407).

16. Timber harvests from national forests in Oregon and Washington declined from 6,974 million board feet in 1988 to 1,424 million in 1993. The total harvest from all lands, public and private, declined 39 percent over the same period. See Warren (1994, table 16).

17. From 1988 through 1994 the resident population of the United States increased 6.48 percent. The comparable figures for Oregon and Washington are 12.59 and 15.15 percent. Over the same period, per capita personal income for the United States increased 32.2 percent in current dollars. Oregon and Washington, which had the same growth in per capita income, increased 37.2 percent (U.S. Department of Commerce 1989 and 1995).

18. For this reason, counting jobs appears to be a favorite ploy of environmental groups interested in showing that preservation pays. See, for example, the Wilderness Society publication by Rasker, Tirrell, and Kloepfer (1992).

19. The value of old-growth or relatively mature timber can be especially high in the export market. Thus, complete restrictions on the exportation of logs from public lands, enacted in conjunction with restriction on harvests because of spotted owl protection, ended up being especially costly. See Johnson, Rucker, and Lippke (1995).

20. Montgomery, Brown, and Adams's (1994) estimates of survivability are based on early estimates of spotted owl populations. Both the range and the size of spotted owl populations have since been shown to be much greater (Chase 1995, 365).

21. It has been argued that many of the recent improvements in environmental quality are the result of regulations (Arrow et al. 1995). Indeed, many of them are. Air pollution is often a transboundary problem involving third-party effects. In such a setting, the cost of contracting among many private entities to obtain a level of pollution that maximizes aggregate net benefits can be prohibitively high. The presence of these third-party effects, often referred to as *externalities*, may justify a regulatory approach. Although the term *externality* is not without ambiguity, it generally implies a condition where the right to contract is absent. That usually means that either property rights are absent or they are ill defined (Cheung 1970). Regulations, however, do not arise in a vacuum. They evolve through the political process, which is conducive to special-interest groups who pressure for favorable legislation. If the demand for a healthy environment increases with income, as is likely, political support for regulations should also increase with income. Although the Clean Air Act and Clean Water Act have clearly contributed to the improvement in ambient conditions, regulations

aimed at improving health have often been costly because of the imposition of excessively high standards relative to the benefits (Viscusi 1993; Van Houtven and Cropper 1996).

22. Encouraging work has been done on valuing biodiversity for use in pharmaceutical research. See Simpson, Sedjo, and Reid (1996). Their approach is to value the marginal species on the basis of its contribution to the probability of making a commercial discovery. Even under very favorable assumptions, the marginal value of a species to pharmaceutical firms undertaking biodiversity prospecting is low. This is in contrast to the claims made by proponents of preservation.

23. See U.S. Department of Agriculture, *Forest Service Manual*, chapter 1970. The wording there makes it clear that benefit-cost analysis is to be an integral part of the planning process. But economic efficiency is to be considered along with "other" factors. The other factors are not specified.

24. Interest in these possibilities is underscored by the popularity of a book by David Osborne and Ted Gaebler, *Reinventing Government*, where the authors call for the adoption of total quality management (TQM) and related practices. Osborne and Gaebler (1992, 129–30) label the government bureaucracy as "bankrupt" and seek to replace it with a more performance-oriented structure: "The task is less to reform civil service than to define the appropriate personnel system for a modern government and create it."

25. Indeed, "no section is more important for TQM to succeed" than the nature of the reward and compensation structure (Johnson 1993, 175). Similar emphasis on the rewards system is noted by Levine (1995, 48), who comments that "some kind of sharing of rewards from involvement is a key element of almost all participatory programs."

26. Although additional performance measures are generally seen as improving outcomes, the opposite can occur if an organization lacks a clear objective (Baker 1992). If an organization is uncertain of its objective, then basing compensation on some narrowly defined criteria could, ex post, send the wrong signals to employees.

27. See, for example, Alston Chase's (1995, 365) comments on the unwillingness of federal biologists to change their claims that the spotted owl was in deep decline even in the face of mounting evidence to contrary.

28. The current federal civil service, with all its faults, is in large part the outcome of conscious decisions over the last one hundred years by the president and Congress to limit competition over control of the bureaucracy (Johnson and Libecap 1994). It also has been molded in an important way by the effective lobbying efforts of federal employee unions to add attributes to the system in their behalf. Because Congress, the president, and federal labor unions all have a stake in the current arrangement, significantly changing the structure of the federal civil service is unlikely. One of the few management tools left to the

Clinton administration is to downsize the federal work force, not reinvent it. It has, in fact, begun to accomplish that objective. Total federal civilian employment declined 7.2 percent between January 1992 and January 1996 (U.S. Office of Personnel Management 1996).

29. The changing composition of federal jobs illustrates the pattern. In 1980, for example, 17 percent of total General Schedule employment was in professional occupations. By 1993, the proportion had risen to 23 percent. Over the same period, the proportion of administrative employees increased from 20 to 26 percent (U.S. Office of Personnel Management 1994, 13).

30. Empirical evidence on the discretionary behavior of bureaucrats is beginning to accumulate. See, for example, the papers in the volume on reinventing government edited by Gary Libecap (1996). It is also becoming abundantly clear that federal agencies are less efficient (more costly) at managing natural resources than many state agencies. See, for example, Donald Leal (1995).

31. Data on employment by occupation and selected agencies are available from the Office of Personnel Management.

32. The actions of these employees are supported by environmental groups. See the discussion offered by Schneider (1992). Also see Chase (1995).

References

Anderson, Terry L., and Donald R. Leal. 1991. *Free Market Environmentalism.* Boulder, Colo.: Westview Press.

Arrow, Kenneth, et al. 1995. "Economic Growth, Carrying Capacity, and the Environment." *Science* 268: 520–21.

Avery, Dennis T. 1995. *Saving the Planet with Pesticides and Plastic: The Environmental Triumph of High-Yield Farming.* Indianapolis, Ind.: Hudson Institute.

Baker, George P. 1992. "Incentive Contracts and Performance Measurement." *Journal of Political Economy* 100: 598–614.

Barnett, Harold, and Chandler Morse. 1963. *Scarcity and Growth: The Economics of Natural Resource Availability.* Baltimore, Md.: Johns Hopkins University Press.

Bolsinger, Charles L., and Karen L. Waddell. 1993. *Area of Old-Growth Forests in California, Oregon, and Washington.* PNW-RB-197. Portland, Oreg.: U.S. Forest Service, Pacific Northwest Research Station.

Bridgman, Percy W. 1936. *The Nature of Physical Theory.* New York: Dover Publications.

Brown, Gardner M., and Barry Field. 1978. "Implications of Alternative Measures of Natural Resource Scarcity." *Journal of Political Economy* 86: 229–44.

Carson, Rachel. 1962. *Silent Spring.* Boston: Houghton Mifflin.

Chase, Alston. 1995. *In a Dark Wood: The Fight over Forests and the Rising Tyranny of Ecology.* Boston: Houghton Mifflin.

Cheung, Steven N. S. 1970. "The Structure of a Contract and the Theory of a Non-Exclusive Resource." *Journal of Law and Economics* 13: 49–70.

Cole H. S. D., Christopher Freeman, Marie Jahoda, and K. L. R. Pavitt, eds. 1973. *Models of Doom: A Critique of the Limits to Growth.* New York: Universe Books.

Commoner, Barry. 1971. *The Closing Circle.* New York: Bantam.

Craighead, Frank. 1979. *Track of the Grizzly.* San Francisco: Sierra Club Books.

Daly, Herman E. 1977. *Steady-State Economics: The Economics of Biophysical Equilibrium and Moral Growth.* San Francisco: W. H. Freeman.

Dana, Samuel T., and Sally K. Fairfax. 1980. *Forest and Range Policy.* New York: McGraw-Hill.

Fitzsimmons, Allan K. 1994. "Federal Ecosystem Management: A 'Train Wreck' in the Making." *Policy Analysis* 217.

Food and Agricultural Organization of the United Nations. (Various years). *FAO Yearbook: Production.* Rome: United Nations.

Frentz, Irene, Paul Hardy, Sussane Maleki, Ali Phillips, and Barbara Thorpe. 1995. "Ecosystem Management in the U.S.: An Inventory and Assessment of Current Experience." Department of Natural Resources and Environment, University of Michigan.

Gore, Albert. 1993. *From Red Tape to Results: Creating a Government That Works Better and Costs Less: Report of the National Performance Review.* Washington, D.C.: U.S. Government Printing Office.

Grossman, Gene M., and Alan B. Krueger. 1995. "Economic Growth and the Environment." *Quarterly Journal of Economics* 110: 353–78.

Grumbine, Edward R. 1994. "What Is Ecosystem Management?" *Conservation Biology* 8: 27–38.

Heywood, V. H., ed. 1995. *Global Biodiversity Assessment.* United Nations Environment Programme. Cambridge, Eng.: Cambridge University Press.

Hutchinson, G. Evelyn. 1948. "Circular Causal Systems in Ecology." *Annuals of the New York Academy of Sciences* 50: 221–46.

———. 1978. *An Introduction to Population Ecology.* New Haven, Conn.: Yale University Press.

Johnson, Richard S. 1993. *TQM Leadership for the Quality Transformation.* ASQC Total Quality Management Series. Milwaukee, Wis.: ASQC Press.

Johnson, Ronald N., and Gary D. Libecap. 1994. *The Federal Civil Service System and the Problem of Bureaucracy: The Economics and Politics of Institutional Change.* Chicago: University of Chicago Press.

Johnson, Ronald N., Randal R. Rucker, and Holly Lippke. 1995. "Expanding U.S.

50

Ronald N. Johnson

Log Export Restrictions: Impacts on State Revenue and Policy Implications." *Journal of Environmental Economics and Management* 29: 197–213.

Kaufman, Herbert. 1960. *The Forest Ranger.* Baltimore, Md.: Johns Hopkins University Press.

Keiter, Robert B. 1994. "Beyond the Boundary Line: Constructing a Law of Ecosystem Management." *University of Colorado Law Review* 65: 294–334.

Keystone Center. 1996. *The Keystone National Policy Dialogue on Ecosystem Management.* Keystone, Colo.: Keystone Center.

Leal, Donald R. 1995. *Turning a Profit on Public Forests.* PERC Policy series, PS-4. Bozeman, Mont.: Political Economy Research Center.

Leopold, Aldo. 1949. *A Sand County Almanac and Sketches from Here and There.* New York: Oxford University Press.

Levine, David I. 1995. *Reinventing the Workplace: How Business and Employees Can Both Win.* Washington, D.C.: Brookings Institution.

Libecap, Gary D., ed. 1996. *Reinventing Government and the Problem of Bureaucracy.* London: JAI Press Inc.

Mann, Charles C., and Mark L. Plummer. 1995. *Noah's Choice: The Future of Endangered Species.* New York: Alfred A. Knopf.

McCubbins, Matthew D., Roger G. Noll, and Barry R. Weingast. 1989. "Structure and Process, Politics and Policy: Administrative Arrangements and the Political Control of Agencies." *Virginia Law Review* 75: 432–82.

Meadows, Donella H., Dennis L. Meadows, Jergen Randers, and William W. Behrens III. 1972. *The Limits to Growth: A Report for the Club of Rome's Project on the Predicament of Mankind.* New York: Universe Books.

Montgomery, Claire A., Gardner M. Brown Jr., and Darius M. Adams. 1994. "The Marginal Cost of Species Preservation: The Northern Spotted Owl." *Journal of Environmental Economics and Management* 26: 111–28.

Nelson, Robert H. 1995. *Public Lands and Private Rights: The Failure of Scientific Management.* Lanham, Md.: Rowman and Littlefield Publishers.

Olson, Mancur, Jr. 1996. "Big Bills Left on the Sidewalk: Why Some Nations Are Rich, and Others Poor." Distinguished Lecture on Economics in Government. *Journal of Economic Perspectives* 10: 3–24.

Osborne, David, and Ted Gaebler. 1992. *Reinventing Government.* Reading, Mass.: Addison-Wesley.

Popper, Karl. 1965. *The Logic of Scientific Discovery.* New York: Harper Torch-Books.

Rasker, Ray, N. Tirrell, and D. Kloepfer. 1992. *The Wealth of Nature: New Economic Realities in the Yellowstone Region.* Washington, D.C.: Wilderness Society.

Schneider, Paul. 1992. "When a Whistle Blows in the Forest." *Audubon* 94 (January/February): 42–49.

Sedjo, Roger A. 1995. "Local Logging: Global Effects." *Journal of Forestry* 93: 25–28.

Sedjo, Roger A., and Kenneth S. Lyon. 1990. *The Long-Term Adequacy of World Timber Supply.* Washington, D.C.: Resources for the Future.

Selden, Thomas M., and Daqing Song. 1994. "Environmental Quality and Development: Is There a 'Kuznets Curve' for Air Pollution Emissions?" *Journal of Environmental Economics and Management* 27: 19–34.

Simpson, David R., Roger A. Sedjo, and John W. Reid. 1996. "Valuing Biodiversity for Use in Pharmaceutical Research." *Journal of Political Economy* 104: 163–85.

South Florida Water Management District. 1995. *South Florida Ecosystem Restoration Plan.* West Palm Beach, Fla.: South Florida Water Management District.

Stanley, Thomas R. 1995. "Ecosystem Management and the Arrogance of Humanism." *Conservation Biology* 9: 255–62.

Stroup, Richard L. 1995. *The Endangered Species Act: Making Innocent Species the Enemy.* PERC Policy series, PS-3. Bozeman, Mont.: Political Economy Research Center.

Task Force (Interagency Ecosystem Management Task Force). *The Ecosystem Approach: Healthy Ecosystems and Sustainable Economies.* Vol. 1. Washington, D.C.: Task Force.

U.S. Department of Agriculture. 1996. *Forest Service Manual,* chap. 1970. Washington, D.C.: U.S. Government Printing Office.

U.S. Department of Commerce. Bureau of the Census. (Various years). *Statistical Abstract of the United States.* Washington, D.C.: U.S. Government Printing Office.

U.S. Environmental Protection Agency. 1994. *National Air Pollutant Emission Trends: 1900–1993.* Washington, D.C.: U.S. Government Printing Office.

U.S. Forest Service. Pacific Northwest Region. 1992. *Final Environmental Impact Statement on the Management for the Northern Spotted Owl in the National Forests.* Vols. 1 and 2. Portland, Oreg.: U.S. Forest Service.

U.S. General Accounting Office. 1994. *Ecosystem Management: Additional Actions Needed to Adequately Test a Promising Approach.* GAO/RCED-49-111. Washington, D.C.: U.S. Government Printing Office.

U.S. Office of Personnel Management. 1994. *The Fact Book: Federal Civil Workforce, 1994 Edition.* Washington, D.C.: U.S. Government Printing Office.

———. 1996. *Federal Civilian Workforce Statistics.* Washington, D.C.: U.S. Government Printing Office.

Van Houtven, George, and Maureen L. Cropper. 1996. "When Is a Life Too Costly to Save? The Evidence from U.S. Environmental Regulations." *Journal of Environmental Economics and Management* 30: 348–68.

Viscusi, Kip W. 1993. "The Value of Risks to Life and Health." *Journal of Economic Literature* 31: 1912–46.

Warren, Debra D. 1994. *Production, Prices, Employment, and Trade in Northwest Forest Industries: Third Quarter 1994.* PNW-RB. Portland, Oreg.: U.S. Forest Service, Pacific Northwest Forest and Range Experiment Station.

Weitzman, Martin L. 1992. "On Diversity." *Quarterly Journal of Economics* 107: 363–405.

Wilson, Edward O. 1988. *Biodiversity.* Washington, D.C.: National Academy Press.

Rekindling the Privatization Fires: Political Lands Revisited

In every great monarchy in Europe the sale of the crown lands would produce a very large sum of money, which, if applied to the payment of the public debts, would deliver from mortgage a much greater revenue than any which those lands have ever afforded to the crown. . . . When the crown lands had become private property, they would, in the course of a few years, become well improved and well cultivated.

—*Adam Smith*
The Wealth of Nations

Introduction

More than a decade after the Sagebrush Rebels sent a message to the Washington establishment and the incoming Reagan administration that they were upset with the management of political lands,[1] talk of privatizing federal lands has all but disappeared from the halls of the Capitol. The appointment of James Watt as secretary of the interior seemed to placate western commodity interests including ranchers, loggers, and oil producers. Environmentalists, in contrast, were outraged at

The authors wish to thank the Earhart Foundation for supporting this research and Holly Lippke Fretwell for her research assistance.

this appointment because they feared the rape and ruin of political lands. In the end little changed except that the ranks and coffers of environmental groups grew in response to their concerns.

There is growing dissatisfaction among users and taxpayers alike with Washington's current "formula" for doing business on political lands. Major laws passed in the 1970s that require "democraticizing" public land use through public review have served only to foster protracted legal battles and environmental studies, thereby raising the costs of doing business to prohibitive levels. From this dilemma have come desperate attempts to unlock the logjam of political gridlock as in the case of the spotted owl and salvage timber sales.

If there is one difference in Washington today, it is that people on all sides of the debate recognize that *incentives matter* on political as well as on private lands. That a 1992 Congressional Research Service workshop on multiple-use management included a section on market incentives demonstrates the overarching concern for changing the incentives (Anderson 1992). Congress has *inched* a step closer in this regard with various legislative proposals to address problems of "below-cost" timber and grazing. There are also various proposals to generate income by raising fees for recreation (Coffin 1996). With respect to private land, there is a growing consensus in Congress that landowners must be compensated for the costs incurred in providing endangered species habitat.[2]

The seeds of reform and common ground are being planted using the economic way of thinking. Environmental groups have begun relying on economics to make their case against policies that encourage environmental destruction at taxpayer expense. Groups such as the Wilderness Society and the Sierra Club, for example, have called for an end to timber practices on national forests that drain money from the U.S. Treasury. Similarly, the Environmental Defense Fund has supported water marketing as a win-win approach for replacing the federal water subsidies that have wreaked far more environmental damage than private water interests ever could. Such approaches provide a strong basis for coalescing the interests of environmentalists and fiscal conservatives.

By the same token, there is a recognition that economics can help commodity users make their own strong case against management of political lands. Comparisons of political lands with nearby state and county lands (where the purpose is to generate income) show that a lack of income incentives on political lands is leading not only to rising management costs but also to resource waste.

From both sides of the table, there is a small but growing contingent calling for an end to subsidized public recreation using the power of economics to make their case. Economics of past and present cases of outdoor recreation indicates a far greater willingness to pay for such goods than is currently allowed. Such subsidized public recreation is fostering amenity overuse and abuse.

On the side of private land management, more and more evidence suggests that ecology and markets can function well together (Anderson and Leal 1991). Seeing how the Audubon Society has successfully managed its Rainey Wildlife Sanctuary for both wildlife preservation and gas production (Baden and Stroup 1981) has led researchers to examine other examples of environmentally compatible development (Council on Environmental Quality 1984). In addition to the compatibility of environmental quality and commodity production, there is growing evidence that private lands can provide substantial environmental amenities and outdoor recreation at a profit instead of a loss.

Despite this evidence, there remains opposition to commodity production on environmentally sensitive political lands. The Audubon Society, while extracting natural gas from beneath its privately owned sanctuary, has joined other environmental groups in opposing oil development in the Arctic National Wildlife Refuge (ANWR). The best explanation for such a reaction is that in the political arena the game is zero-sum. If development is allowed, the environmental groups gain nothing and potentially lose; if development is not allowed these groups retain their pristine lands without bearing any opportunity cost. As a result, political management often results in a paralysis and hence the status quo. Although this works to the benefit of environmental interests in cases like ANWR, it also has contributed to the mismanagement of wildlife populations and other resources in the "crown jewel" of our national park system, Yellowstone National Park. The reason is because politicians and bureaucrats have been "playing God" with one of our most treasured gifts (Chase 1986). The lesson is clear: Political management is not always a formula for environmental protection.

In light of the persistent gridlock over the management of political lands and the growing recognition that incentives matter, it is time to rethink political land management, considering innovative solutions from privatization to establishing profit centers. If we are not willing to turn lands over to private managers, at least we must try to get the incentives right for political managers. We must ask why billions of dollars worth of public land are a liability to the government rather than an asset. What institutional changes would it take to convert those lands that are a drain on the treasury into fiscal assets? That is the central question addressed in this chapter.

The First Privatization Movement

In contrast to today, when there is only lip service paid to the disposal of political lands, the first one hundred years following the American Revolution witnessed a land policy aimed at turning the political domain into private ownership. Of course, during these first years the domain of the federal government was growing rapidly. States were ceding their western lands to the newly formed federal government, and new territories such as the Louisiana Purchase were helping fulfill our "manifest destiny."

During the period following ratification of the Constitution, the Federalists, led mainly by Hamilton, believed that a limited democratic government would function best if power were fragmented, and fragmentation meant private ownership. Jefferson in particular is famous for his insistence that the nation be populated by yeoman farmers owning their lands. Hamilton's support of public lands being disposed into private hands was more pragmatic; for him the political domain represented a vast resource base that could provide badly needed revenue for the infant government with large debts. For these first privatizers, the main function of government was to set policies for disposing of the political domain.

Although the Continental Congress was bankrupt after the war, it did have enormous tracts of land ceded it by the newly formed states, and leaders were reluctant to give away the land. "The public land was

Table 1   Receipts from the Public Domain, 1787–1840

Year	Nominal Receipts	Real Receipts*
Before June 1796	$ 1,201,726	$ 8,020,931
1796–1799	99,340	704,486
1800–1805	1,550,195	10,993,466
1806–1810	3,018,149	1,859,105
1811–1815	5,010,251	2,485,513
1816–1820	11,226,071	82,179,668
1821–1825	6,133,580	56,428,936
1826–1830	7,754,470	79,988,533
1831–1835	29,417,081	317,891,250
1836–1840	46,157,758	498,796,852

* 1987 dollars
SOURCE: Donaldson (1970, 17).

proposed as a means of debt liquidation. In 1782, Jefferson estimated
that 5,000,000 acres could readily be sold at a dollar per acre in government debt certificates and the whole national debt soon paid with the
proceeds from additional sales" (Sakolski 1932, 33). Surely, Hamilton
was overly optimistic about the potential of land sales during the early
years of the republic, but, as table 1 suggests, disposal of the political
domain in exchange for cash, certificates, public debt, and land warrants
did generate significant revenues. In the absence of privatization
through land sales, it is highly unlikely that the government could have
retired its massive debt by 1835, which it did manage to do.

The Leftovers

The mood of the country regarding disposal of the political domain had
changed dramatically by the Progressive Era in the late nineteenth century. After the debt was retired in 1835, disposal policy shifted away from
wholesale disposal to speculators, who in turn sold the land to settlers,
toward retail giveaways under the Preemption and Homestead Acts.
Through the wholesale and retail disposal policies, over a billion acres
of political lands were privatized between 1790 and 1920.

58

Terry L. Anderson and Donald R. Leal

Table 2   Federal Land (in thousands of acres)

Agency (year) [a]	Total	Alaska Only	Eleven Western States
Forest Service [b] (1994)	191,602	22,053	141,028
Fish and Wildlife Service [c] (1995)	92,349	76,787	7,468
Bureau of Land Management [d] (1993)	267,640	88,860	162,993
Park Service [e] (1995)	83,183	54,645	20,633
All other	18,860	5,695	22,102
Total federal [d] (1990)	649,802	248,040	354,224
Total area (1990) (excluding inland water)	2,271,343	365,481	752,948

[a] Years are different because of data availability. It should be noted, however, that totals vary little over time.

[b] U.S. Department of Agriculture (1994).

[c] U.S. Fish and Wildlife Service (1995).

[d] U.S. Department of the Interior (1994).

[e] Data provided by U.S. Department of Interior, National Park Service, Land Resources Division, "Master Deed Listing," 12/31/95.

Despite this, reservation rather than disposal of the political domain began dominating land policy by the turn of the century. The Progressives believed that there was ample evidence that good resource stewardship would not come from private owners guided by the invisible hand of the market. They believed market failure had been demonstrated by the "rape and run" tactics of timber companies in the Great Lakes region and mining companies in the West. Because of such failures, management by governmental "professionals" should replace decentralized private control. Proponents of government ownership such as Gifford Pinchot and John Muir argued that timber famines would result from private ownership, that private ownership did not encourage the longer view, that conservation was only possible with political management, and that multiple-use management would not exist on private lands. These arguments still dominate the modern debates for retention of the political domain.[3]

Out of the Progressive Era, nearly one-third of the nation's land was reserved under federal control[4] (see table 2). Not surprisingly, because most of the initial privatization took place in the eastern half of the

Table 3   Commodity Lands in the Forty-Eight Contiguous States, 1980 (in thousands of acres)

Surface Use	NATIONAL FOREST		Public Lands [a]	Total
	Eastern	Western		
Commercial forest	20,786	61,404	4,141	86,331
Grazing [b]	407	36,659	149,514	186,580
Total	21,193	98,063	153,655	272,911

[a] Includes 421,000 acres in the eastern states.

[b] Does not include grazing that occurs on commercial forest land.

SOURCE: Estimates for 1980 based on U.S. Forest Service (1980), U.S. Department of the Interior (1981), and agency estimates of area of designated wilderness, which are not included in totals.

United States, the percentage of federal control is greatest in the eleven western states and Alaska. When Alaska is excluded from the data, 22 percent of the United States is still federally managed. (These figures do not include an estimated 1.4 billion acres of outer continental shelf seafloor lands controlled by the Department of the Interior.)

Table 3 shows the commodity-producing lands in the lower forty-eight states in 1980. Note that the total of 650 million acres declines dramatically once Alaska lands, dedicated lands, parks, refuges, and so on are subtracted. Nonetheless, of the approximately 400 million acres of federal lands in the forty-eight contiguous states, nearly 70 percent, or 272,911,000 acres, are commodity-producing lands. These are the lands that ought to be profit centers.

To get a rough idea of the total value of these assets, let us assume that they would bring $500 per acre for the commodity values alone if they were sold at auction. (In reality, as will be discussed later, many of the commodity-producing lands may be more valuable for recreational and environmental amenities.) Liquidation of these assets under this assumption would generate more than $136 billion, approximately 4 percent of the national debt. Adding in Forest Service and Bureau of Land Management lands in Alaska (excluding the 67.7 million acres for Alaskan Native Americans), and assuming that they would only be worth half as much per acre, revenues from land sales would generate another $24 billion.

These figures, of course, do not take into account the expenditure impact of the agencies that manage the political lands. Net costs associated with timber and grazing on Forest Service lands amounted to approximately $235 million in 1994.[5] Amortizing these costs over fifty years at 5 percent yields present-value savings of more than $52 billion. Add in recreation and fish and wildlife losses, and the present value of costs to the taxpayer comes to $113 billion.

These numbers are not meant to predict how much revenue the sale of political lands would generate. They are simply meant to suggest that the federal government has a significant part of its portfolio tied up in political lands that continually incur losses for the treasury. If any private owner managed an asset as poorly as the U.S. Forest Service manages its lands, he would soon be bankrupt. Furthermore, in incurring such large losses, the Forest Service ignores many other values associated with its lands because of perverse incentives. Privatizing the commodity-producing lands would remove these perverse incentives by making managers incur the full cost of their decisions and encourage more efficient land management.

Is There Market Failure?

Opponents of privatization and advocates of maintaining the status quo argue that market failure would lead to underprovision of recreational and environmental amenities. As Roderick Nash, a wilderness historian, asserts, "without formal [government] preservation the remaining American wilderness would vanish" (Nash 1976, 26 and 126–27). The culprit is perceived to be the free enterprise system, and only the political land system can compensate for its shortcomings. With widespread acceptance of the market failure argument, it is much easier to make the case for political management and even for expanding the federal estate. For example, in 1987 the President's Commission on American Outdoors (PCAO), charged with reviewing "outdoor recreation policies, programs and opportunities" for both the public and the private sectors, recommended expanding the federal estate for recreation and amenity production. Its recommendations led to the establishment of the Land

and Water Conservation Fund used to purchase some 2.8 million acres for federal agencies during the period from 1965 to 1982 (Conservation Foundation 1985, 283). The commission called for a $15 billion trust fund that would generate "an absolute minimum" of $1 billion to acquire, develop, and protect open space; a nationwide network of public greenways connecting existing and new parks, forests, and other open spaces; and, finally, a scenic byways project that would require an expenditure of $200 million a year to protect scenic views along roadways through restrictive zoning. In the words of William K. Reilly (1987, xi), then president of the Conservation Foundation and later director of the Environmental Protection Agency (EPA), the commission has "affirmed a crucial federal role in funding, leadership, and resource husbandry." When the PCAO report was released, a dismayed Jacqueline Schaefer, a member of the President's Council on Environmental Quality (CEQ), pointed out that the commission did not emphasize people and the ways they create opportunities. She interpreted the report as saying that "you can't have [recreational] opportunity unless you have land guaranteed by the government."

Is there market failure leading to a bias against private provision of recreational and environmental amenities and requiring political provision? The private calculus for land use is expressed by a familiar saying among farmers and ranchers: "If it pays, it stays." In short, private producers must face the reality check of profits and losses. Thus, the important public policy questions are, Do markets for privately provided recreational services and environmental amenities accurately reflect the values to consumers and the costs to producers? Can providing recreational and environmental amenities pay? In all cases the answer will depend on the nature of property rights to inputs and outputs.

A market for any good including recreation requires two elements: (1) there must be a demand for it (i.e., consumers are willing to pay for it) and (2) there must be a way for producers to capture the benefits from producing it. If recreation is simply a by-product from other production and there is no market for it, there will be little incentive to focus on producing recreational opportunities.

Cattle ranching provides an example. Meat consumers are willing to pay the price that makes it profitable to use land for ranching. With well-defined and enforced rights to land, the producer can run the enterprise with some expectation that he can claim the rewards. Fencing defines the ownership of land and water resources, and a brand identifies ownership of the cattle. There is also the force of the law to protect and defend the producer's claim. Along with cattle production come other benefits, such as open space and wildlife habitat, and other costs, such as stream bank erosion and overgrazing of wildlife ranges. These goods and bads, however, will not weigh heavily in the rancher's calculus except to the extent that he "cares" about these amenities, and in most cases this "land ethic," as Aldo Leopold called it, is important. Nonetheless, environmental protection is an example of market failure to the extent property rights to the amenities are not well defined and enforced or not valuable to people who demand them.

To understand the potential for market failure in recreational production, consider the case of elk habitat and hunting access. For elk hunting to be a profitable venture, there must be enough hunters willing to pay for it and there must be a way of excluding those who do not pay. Understandably, if there is uncertainty in controlling the resources and claiming the returns, few private landowners would incur costs to provide elk habitat.

Opponents of private wildlife management argue that, in the absence of government ownership, "commercialism" would lead to the extermination of species as it did with buffalo, swans, and passenger pigeons. "The tragedy of the commons" (Hardin 1968), however, more accurately explains the demise of buffalo, swans, and other animal species; no one owned these wildlife resources so no one had an incentive to husband them. Property rights were not established until the buffalo were dead. Historically, wildlife exploitation can be linked to a lack of private property rights and an absence of markets, not the other way around.

When landowners can market the wildlife and environmental amenities on their property, views of wildlife can change dramatically, but if they cannot, such amenities may become liabilities. Rancher Michael Curran's situation points to some of the factors that influence decisions to produce wildlife and habitat: "We feed 250 elk for six months, and 500 deer and about 300 antelope for an entire year. . . . We've figured that if the Montana Fish and Game Department paid us for the forage consumed, they'd owe us $6,500 every year" (Blood and Baden 1984,

13). Because deer, antelope, and elk are often a costly nuisance, one rancher in Wyoming went so far as to construct a six-foot-high, twenty-seven-mile-long antelope-proof fence to protect his range for livestock (National Wildlife Federation 1984, 8–9).

What Are the Impediments to Private Provision?

In some cases there may be technological barriers to establishing property rights, but when resources become scarce there is an incentive for people to overcome the barriers. In the early settlement of the United States, for example, prairie grass was up for grabs in the commons. The low value of grazing land (given its initial abundance) did not make it worth incurring the high cost of fencing. As grazing values eventually rose and fencing costs declined with the invention of barbed wire, however, privatization became feasible. Today we take this fencing technology for granted, but it evolved in response to the rising value of grazing land. Although fencing may not provide a solution to establishing property rights to wildlife,[6] the important point is that, as the value of the resource rises, more effort will be put into overcoming the tragedy of the commons.

It is not a lack of entrepreneurship that is preventing more recreation opportunities and protection of environmental amenities. As values of amenities rise, private entrepreneurs will make efforts to capitalize on profit opportunities by establishing property rights. One main reason there are not more attempts is the government's distortion of values.

Because most services provided by the government are not fully paid for by the user, governmental (political) prices generally are lower than private-sector prices for the same good or service. With respect to recreation, the most obvious cases include token fees to national parks and public campgrounds and free hiking and hunting in public areas. The entrance fee for a seven-day stay in Yellowstone Park, for example, was raised in 1987 from $2.00, where it had been since the Park Service assumed management responsibility in 1912, to $5 a vehicle and then again in 1988 to $10. Adjusting the 1912 price for inflation results in a price in 1987 dollars of nearly $100! Not only is the current entrance fee far below the real price in 1912, it is far below that of alternative recreation. Comparing revenues from entrance fees alone, Disney World collects, on average, $46 a visitor while Yellowstone collects $1.32 a visitor (O'Toole 1995, 27; Foldvary 1994, 126).

Similarly, the fee for camping at a public campground is much lower than the fee charged at a private campground. In Yellowstone, for example, an overnight stay costs $6 a vehicle versus $15 to $31 (depending on the size of the party and facilities used) at nearby private campgrounds.[7] The private operations do not have the luxury of taxpayers picking up the tab for such items as land, roads, toilets, water outlets, labor, trash removal, and maintenance. To counter the price disparity and attract customers, however, private campgrounds often provide additional facilities including shower units and electrical and water hookups for recreational vehicles.

This subsidized competition is especially prevalent in the West. Where there are extensive federal land holdings, the prices of hunting, fishing, backpacking, and camping are low. Timber companies with large land holdings in the West could provide significant recreational opportunities, but it is difficult to compete with the unrealistically low or zero government prices. As a result, they have spent little or nothing to enforce their property rights in amenities and have tended to ignore these values in management decisions.

The story is much different in the East and South, however, where most of the land is privately owned. In these regions timber companies carry out many programs to improve wildlife populations and habitat and enhance recreational opportunities. In the absence of subsidized recreational opportunities, these companies can charge user fees that make it worth defining and enforcing property rights.

The International Paper (IP) Company's wildlife program is a prime example of establishing new property rights and hence new incentives. IP employs wildlife specialists to oversee wildlife and recreation on its lands, including the 16,000-acre Southlands Experiment Forest located near Bainbridge, Georgia, where research is carried out to develop forest management practices that enhance wildlife populations as well as profits (Lueck 1983, 12). White-tailed deer, turkeys, rabbits, bobwhite quail, mourning doves, and other species are beginning to reap the benefits of new management techniques, as are International Paper and hunters.

Habitat is improved by controlled burning, buffer zones along streams, and tree-cutting practices that leave wildlife cover and plenty of forage (Council on Environmental Quality 1984, 426).

According to company officials, investing in wildlife research and habitat production makes sound business sense. On its 1.65 million acres in the southeastern United States, IP charges eighty-three cents an acre for hunting clubs and sixty-two cents an acre for individual hunters. Company officials see the return going as high as $10 an acre in the future as more hunters seek the good hunting conditions available on IP lands. International Paper's 3,500-acre Cherokee Game Management Area in East Texas already earns $6 an acre annually. For the nation's largest private landowner, $10 an acre is a considerable incentive (Blood and Baden 1984, 11). Indeed, in the southeast region, the company earns 25 percent of its profits from recreation.

The fee hunting alternative is evident in Texas, where more than 85 percent of the land is privately owned. Deer hunters purchase leases ranging from $100 to $2,000, depending on the quality and quantity of the game and the facilities and services offered by the landowner. Leases vary; 71 percent are deer season leases, 19 percent are year-round leases, 5 percent are day leases, and 5 percent are short-term leases. The net returns "from deer leases equal or exceed the annual net returns from livestock operations in many areas of the state" (Taylor, Beattie, and Livengood 1980). Thus, the returns are a powerful incentive for landowners to provide the public with good hunting opportunities.

Legal barriers raise the cost of private provision of wildlife and environmental amenities. For example, U.S. common law dictates that wildlife is owned by the public and that the state is therefore empowered to act as guardian or trustee of the wildlife. In other words, the right to regulate hunting and habitat management is not considered the appropriate domain of private landowners.

Despite these barriers to making wildlife habitat a paying proposition on private lands, there are a growing number of examples of private provision of wildlife habitat for both hunting and nonhunting. This list is growing because the value of these alternatives is growing. Consider two examples.

The Flying D Ranch in southwestern Montana encompasses 107,514 deeded acres of steep Douglas fir forests, rolling grass hills, and meadowed stream bottoms. The land was a working cattle ranch until 1989, when it was purchased by media magnate Ted Turner. In return for valuable tax deductions, Turner Enterprises granted conservation easements to the Nature Conservancy, removed the cattle, improved the fences, and converted the Flying D to a bison ranch. By 1993 the ranch was stocked with 3,391 bison raised mainly to stock a growing number of bison ranches and a growing meat market.

The ranch also provides an excellent wildlife habitat, especially for elk and deer, and the streams on the property offer excellent trout fishing. Golden and bald eagles soar overhead, and occasionally grizzly bears, bighorn sheep, and mountain goats pass through.

The value of the wildlife assets was recognized in the 1980s, when the previous owner began actively restricting access and managing hunting. The impact of this management has been dramatic. The elk population has grown from 757 in 1981 to 3,507 in 1994, a 463 percent increase! During the same period, elk herds generally increased in Montana but not by nearly as much. The increase on the Flying D was achieved by restricting the number and size of bulls harvested and by increasing the harvest of cow elk, thus reducing the cow-to-bull ratio. As a result calf crops generally run 50 to 60 percent, and immature bulls (those with fewer than five points on each antler) are numerous. Ranch manager Russ Miller employs a professional hunting guide, Rob Arnaud, who looks after the hunting operation. Miller and Arnaud use a helicopter, fixed-wing aircraft, and observations by ranch employees to establish an extensive database on wildlife populations. Their "Annual Wildlife Report" provides state wildlife officials with data on herd size, harvest data, and age and sex characteristics necessary to control the number and type of elk harvested each year.

Miller is not a hunter, so he sees the wildlife as competitors with his cash crop, bison. Given that elk consume grass that could be eaten by bison, Miller wants the elk to pay their own way and they do. Rob Arnaud's guided elk hunts sell for $8,000 (not including state license fees), and in 1993, his thirty elk hunters harvested twenty-six trophy bulls. The elk hunters were also allowed to hunt mule and white-tailed deer and, if successful, were charged additional trophy fees of $3,500 and $3,000, respectively. Three trophy mule deer bucks and four trophy white-tailed deer bucks were harvested in 1993. To help cull old bulls from the herd, hunters can shoot a bison bull on the Flying D, and in 1993 five hunters did so at a price of $3,500 each.

With gross revenues of approximately $300,000, wildlife on the Flying D is an asset. (This was estimated by us on the basis of data in the ranch's annual wildlife report.) Wildlife is producing income for the ranching enterprise, employment for the guides, and quality trophy hunts for the clients. The public also benefits from Turner's wildlife management. Abundant herds spill over onto adjacent public lands, where access is unrestricted. Moreover, to keep the sex distribution of the herd in balance, Miller and Arnaud work with the Montana Department of Fish, Wildlife, and Parks and allow free access to the Flying D for restricted public hunting of cow elk. In 1993, 189 hunters harvested 101 cow elk. As quoted earlier, "If it pays, it stays." Wildlife is likely to stay on the Flying D.

The wide open spaces of Texas are the setting of another amazing effort to preserve species and provide amenities. Fossil Rim Wildlife Center is located about eighty miles south of Dallas, Texas, and consists of three thousand acres of rolling hills and grasslands. Since the early 1970s, it has been a sanctuary for hard-pressed wildlife from around the globe. Species such as the white rhino, for instance, threatened by poaching in Africa, find safe haven at Fossil Rim. The nearly extinct Attwater's prairie chicken, the rare red wolf, Gravy's zebra, and the scimitar-horned oryx (extinct in the wild) have also found a home at Fossil Rim.

The Fossil Rim staff hopes that these animals are taking their first steps toward recovering in the wild. Research and breeding programs at Fossil Rim focus on saving species before they are lost to future generations and one day repopulating the wild. On board are naturalists and veterinarians helping beleaguered species overcome the specter of extinction.

Fossil Rim's record speaks for itself. Since receiving its first pair of red wolves in 1989, Fossil Rim has had thirteen surviving births, paving the way for successful reintroduction in the wild. Nearly seventy cheetahs have been born at Fossil Rim. This is impressive considering the fact that, worldwide, more cheetahs die than are born every year. Many have been farmed out to other captive breeding programs or zoos so that they will not have to take wild ones for their stocking programs. Fossil Rim has also successfully bred addax antelope into a herd of one hundred, believed to be the largest in the world. Although most of its efforts focus on animals in trouble, Fossil Rim also devotes resources to conservation efforts in native habitats. For example, the center has contributed staff to study habitat needs of the cotton top mararin (a multicolored monkey) in Colombia and donated several trucks to the Chihuahua Bioreserve in Mexico.

The story behind Fossil Rim is one of both altruism and entrepreneurialism. In the early 1970s, oilman Tom Mantzel purchased 1,400 acres of what was then Waterfall Ranch, an exotic game ranch, with the goal of turning it into a sanctuary for a growing list of rare animals. Mantzel renamed it Fossil Rim Wildlife Ranch and began populating it with wildlife until there were about sixteen nonnative or endangered species on the property including five hundred individual animals. Fossil Rim became the first ranch to participate in a species survival plan of the American Association of Zoological Parks and Aquariums. By 1984, however, the U.S. petroleum industry had collapsed and the Texas economy was suffering.

To help fund the operation, Mantzel opened Fossil Rim to the public for a fee. He built a 9.5-mile road through the hills and pastures so the public could drive through and observe the wildlife from a distance. He added a snack bar and a souvenir store. Volunteers guided an ever-increasing number of schoolchildren, scouts, and families through the refuge.

Mounting oil losses forced Mantzel to take on two partners to maintain the facility, Jim Jackson and Christine Jurzykowski. The husband and wife did not come from a conservation background but were looking for a way to make a difference. At first, they supplied funds to keep the ranch operating, but in 1987 they bought Fossil Rim outright.

Under their direction, Fossil Rim has made great strides. It has grown from 1,400 acres to 3,000 acres, and its animal population has increased from five hundred to one thousand animals encompassing thirty-two species. Not all are endangered, but all bring in paying tourists to support the refuge. On the staff are naturalists and veterinarians who carry out a variety of groundbreaking projects. For example, the staff is working to perfect reproductive technologies for a larger gene pool for the addax antelope. They are also carrying out captive breeding research on white rhino, using a "teaser" male in one enclosure that encourages a male in an adjacent enclosure with females to breed. And Fossil Rim researchers are testing techniques for reversible contraception to allow population control of animals in captivity that can be reversed when they enter the wild.

To finance such endeavors, Jackson and Jurzykowski use their entrepreneurial imagination to capitalize on various revenue sources. The big moneymaker is still the drive-through tour, with 95,000 people a year paying $12.95 each. In addition to the 9.5-mile tour, however, they now offer tourists a number of packages. There is the Foothills Safari Camp, packaged especially for "safari" goers. Its six tents accommodate a maximum of twelve adult guests, except on special family weekends when children under eighteen are allowed. This camp is not exactly an African safari of old. Each tent has twin beds, central air conditioning and heat, ceiling fan, private bathroom with shower, Southwestern decor, and a patio with chairs. Meals are taken in a pavilion with large windows for viewing wildlife. Menus include blackened rib-eye steak, chicken with cranberry and peach chutney, as well as delicious desserts. Weather permitting, campers enjoy meals around the campfire. Rates for a three-day safari camp are $450 an adult on weekends and $375 midweek. Rates are lower for children, and singles not assigned a roommate or wanting a tent to themselves pay extra. There is also a bed-and-breakfast lodge at Fossil Rim for the less adventuresome. The facility overlooks hills and meadows filled with wildlife.

Revenues are augmented with individual and foundation donations to make ends meet. In 1992, revenues from tourism topped $2.2 million, while business expenses were somewhat higher, at $2.6 million. The owners hope that by capitalizing on the growing market for ecotourism they can rely solely on visitor fees. Hundreds of people already visit the center every week, and it is gaining attention among ecotourists beyond Texas. Perseverance and imagination by the enviro-capitalists is paying off.

Such success stories are harder to find in the political sector because its funding mechanism is congressional appropriation, not market demand. For example, in national forests, wildlife generates almost no revenues and little budget. In fiscal year 1985, the Forest Service spent $800 million on its timber and timber support programs and an additional $418 million in road construction, for approximately 75 percent of the total appropriated funds. In contrast, approximately $37 million, or 2.3 percent of the total appropriated funds, was spent on wildlife and fish management (Barton and Fosburgh 1986, 34). The reason for this large disparity is that the budgeting system rewards timber, not wildlife, because the timber generates money for the treasury (O'Toole 1988).

Not surprisingly, this budgeting process affects resource management. Removal of security and thermal cover for elk and deer is an unfortunate by-product of logging and road construction in the national forests of the Rocky Mountains. The national forests that surround Yellowstone National Park, for example, provide some of the best opportunities for elk hunting on political land in the contiguous United States, and hunters bring in millions of dollars to the local economies. But because elk values are not reflected in the Forest Service budget, management for hunting is not a major concern. According to state wildlife biologists, the huge swaths of deforested land created from clearcutting and the construction of roads in roadless areas have reduced elk security and increased access in the forest. The result is that mature bull elk harvested in these areas are on the decline (Henkel 1985, 17). Even though all the forests surrounding Yellowstone Park lose money on timber production, at least they generate some revenues for the treasury and for the agency.

Where to from Here?

Certainly there are cases where private landowners will not be able to capture sufficient returns to induce amenity production on private land, but with growing market potential, more could be done to foster private provision. The important question is, how do we reform our institutional structure to move in the direction that harnesses private incentives where possible? What follows are some specific reforms that can move us in that direction. The proposals are given in order (we believe) from most to least politically palatable.

CONTRACTING OUT SERVICES

If land ownership and management must remain in the political sector, cost savings and output quality can often be improved by contracting out to the private sector. For example, campgrounds owned and operated by the U.S. Forest Service can be run for profit by private firms. When such services are contracted out, the quality improves because the profit-maximizing operators have an incentive to determine what the consumers want and are willing to pay for. With the revenues from user fees, additional and improved services can be provided. The U.S. Forest Service is already contracting out campground concessions, so it would not be a major step to expand other services such as wildlife management, stream reclamation, and trail construction and maintenance.

USER FEES

If lands are going to be retained under political control, charge realistic fees for all uses. Commodity uses, such as logging, are auctioned in a competitive process that tends to make the user pay what the commodity is worth. Of course, this is not to say that revenues from these uses cover the full bureaucratic costs. Recreational uses, however, generally are free and therefore cover almost none of their costs. In fact, losses to the federal treasury resulting from recreation can exceed losses from commodities by a margin of two to one. Annual revenues from a park as famous as Yellowstone only amount to approximately $3 million, though operating expenditures are $19 million. Charging realistic user fees would help cover the significant cost of providing recreational and environmental amenities and would make it easier for private-sector alternatives to compete. These fees are easy to collect at national parks and wilderness areas where conventional access points are limited. Where toll collection at an access point is uneconomical, users could be required to carry a recreation permit just as hunters are required to carry a hunting permit. Some might abuse this system by not carrying a permit, but this should not be a significant problem. Just because there are some enforcement costs, realistic fees can still be charged.

LEASING

For the many political lands having little or no commodity value and no special wilderness designation, rights for amenity values could be leased. For example, on Forest Service lands with little timber, grazing, or mineral potential, groups or individuals could be encouraged to establish leases for environmental habitat protection or exclusive hunting and fishing privileges. The leaseholder could choose to set off an area as a sanctuary for wildlife, not allowing any consumptive activities to take place. Or the leaseholder could allow hunting and fishing on a fee basis. The lease could be offered with an option to buy all or part of the land of interest. Groups such as the Rocky Mountain Elk Foundation, the Nature Conservancy, Ducks Unlimited, and Trout Unlimited could use recreational leases as a way to finance their primary goal of bring more acreage under protection for fish and wildlife purposes. Such leases would allow groups to ameliorate crowding problems on political lands where overuse is causing deterioration of the recreational or environmental quality. The lease period could be offered in five-year increments, and as with commodity leases, leaseholders would have options to buy at the end of the period. Although these schemes may not cover all the potential problems inherent in privatizing political lands, they at least offer a way of overcoming the stumbling blocks.

Where commodity lands have been leased, subleasing to noncommodity groups should be allowed. This approach was tried by the Nature Conservancy (TNC), but administrative hurdles stood in the way. TNC has purchased private ranches with grazing permits and attempted not to graze the lands. For example, it purchased an Arizona ranch with the explicit intention of retiring the federal grazing permits, but an administrative law judge ruled that permits are for the expressed purpose of grazing and therefore must be grazed. If they are not, they can be leased to other grazers.

This ruling has tremendous implications for the use of markets to preserve amenity values. By disallowing the sale of grazing permits to nongrazers, the livestock producer has only one incentive—graze the land himself or sell the permits to other grazers. In this system, environmental interests are explicitly excluded from the market. Not surprisingly, TNC has abandoned plans to buy other ranches in the West for the purpose of reducing grazing.

CORPORATIZATION

As Randal O'Toole (1988) has made clear, commodity production on political lands is creating a few thousand forest jobs at a tremendous expense to taxpayers and the environment. Given the incentives for bureaucrats to maximize budgets, these results are very predictable. Therefore he suggests reforming the Forest Service by "corporatizing" it. Under this scheme, the land and resources remain under political ownership, but the managing agency would be required to fund its operation from revenues generated from the commodities and recreational services produced from the resource base. A form of this scheme is being tried in New Zealand, where commodity-producing forests have been placed into a state-owned enterprise (SOE), which is charged with operating the resources for a profit. Although this scheme does not allow the SOE to consider alternative land uses, it does introduce some incentives for efficiency.

ENDOWMENT BOARDS

The endowment board concept, developed by economist Richard Stroup, could be applied to areas requiring protection of unique environmental assets such as wilderness or endangered species habitat. The endowment board would be charged with the responsibility of managing each area with one primary objective: namely, preserving the unique values of the area. Members of the board would be selected from established environmental groups, and final selection would require congressional approval similar to the process involved in selecting Supreme Court judges. Each member of the board would be bound by fiducial responsibility to protect the unique values of the area. An important feature of this concept is the opportunity for board members to decide for themselves on how best to accomplish their objectives. This could entail a decision to allow energy or some other development along with appropriate operational restrictions to occur in a small part of the area.

In this case the board would have the flexibility of choosing other uses as long as the unique values of the area are protected.

The endowment board creates incentives similar to those faced by environmental groups such as the Audubon Society and the Nature Conservancy where they manage privately owned assets. The now classic example of the Rainey Preserve owned by the Audubon Society provides an excellent illustration of the potential of such arrangements. Rainey is a wildlife sanctuary in Louisiana, home not only to wintering waterfowl and several endangered species but also to several revenue-generating gas wells. Audubon took a bold step when it decided to allow an oil company to drill wells in the area, but officials decided that by applying stringent rules for protecting the unique assets of the region such an arrangement was not only feasible, it was also extremely profitable. Audubon has used the millions of dollars in gas royalties to further their mission by acquiring more wildlife habitat. The wilderness board concept is designed to operate similarly by providing board members the opportunity to carefully weigh alternative uses. This is a much-needed replacement for the rigid, no-development approach inherent in current designated federal wilderness areas.

CREATE INCOME TRUST LANDS

Each year at least fifty national forests managed by the Forest Service lose money on their timber sale programs.[8] Although critics claim that below-cost timber programs occur because logging is not economically feasible, Forest Service budget data suggest they occur instead because of agency inefficiencies. Because the Forest Service is under no legal obligation to make a profit, it has little incentive to keep its costs low. Indeed, budgetary incentives currently in place actually encourage excessive spending.

In contrast, the timber sale program carried out on the forests of Montana's state school trust lands[9] provides an excellent illustration of how different incentives can encourage efficiency and environmental quality. Logging sites on school trust lands are often located next to or even within national forests. Their climate, topography, and variety of trees are similar, and there are important operational similarities. Like the Forest Service, the Department of State Lands (DSL), the state agency charged with care and management of trust lands, must prepare timber sales, administer harvests, carry out environmental assessments, respond to environmental appeals, and conduct competitive bids for timber. Like the Forest Service, the DSL requires road construction, tree stand improvement, and reforestation. It must also integrate its timber activities with other uses such as public recreation, wildlife habitat, livestock grazing, and special-use leases.

Where these agencies differ markedly is in the stated purpose for the use of their lands. State forests are mandated by law to generate income from timber (and other uses) for the funding of public schools. National forests have no such mandate. By law, national forests are managed to achieve the "combination [of land uses] that will best meet the needs of the American people . . . and not necessarily the combination of uses that will give the greatest dollar return or the greatest unit output."[10]

A comparison of federal forests with Montana state forests shows that the Forest Service could make money selling timber from some of its money-losing forests if it operated as efficiently as the state. Montana averages two dollars in revenue for every dollar it spends, while the U.S. Forest Service averages only fifty cents in revenue for every dollar it spends. Moreover, there is no reason to sacrifice environmental quality. Montana's environmental protection is every bit as good as the Forest Service's, as the 1992 environmental audit of Montana forests indicates. In addition, the state does a better job of sustaining quality timber, that is, trees that are alive and free of disease.

Why is the Forest Service's performance so much poorer than the performance of the state of Montana? First, the state has a clear purpose: maximizing returns from its investments in timber and other goods and services marketed from state lands. This requires maintaining the future capacity and environmental quality of the land. The Forest Service has no such incentive. Second, because returns on investments in timber production are earmarked for public schools, school districts have a vested interest in monitoring state land management to ensure that it meets these objectives.

Incentives similar to those for managers of state school trust lands could be created by legally mandating that federal land managers maximize returns from investments in timber and other uses and earmark them for special purposes. For example, suppose that net returns from national forest management were earmarked for Social Security or for county governments. This would create vested interest groups with legal standing and a powerful incentive to monitor land managers, and managers would face a bottom line.

PRIVATIZATION

The least politically feasible but most effective way to create market discipline for land management is to move ownership from the political sector to the private sector. Of course, rekindling the privatization fires raises several important political issues. First, there will be opposition to privatization from user groups accustomed to free or artificially low-priced uses of political lands. Second, there is the question of which political lands to privatize and when. Because the outputs for commodity-producing lands are marketed, the nearly 273 million political acres having mainly commodity value would be much easier to transfer to private ownership than those having primarily environmental value. Finally, there is the question of how to incorporate noncommodity values such as recreation and wildlife habitat into the disposal process. Let us consider these issues in turn.

The issue of political resistance cannot be taken lightly. In 1982 the Reagan administration recommended the sale of a modest 35 million acres, or 5 percent, of the federal estate. It was the most visible effort at outright divestiture of government property since the first privatization movement ended in the 1920s. But despite the modest amount of land to be sold, the disposal program was unceremoniously canceled only a year later. Those with hopes for the program failed to anticipate the opposition from not only environmentalists but also developmental interests such as grazing and logging. Indeed, the controversy generated over the proposed program "reflected a sense that the debate concerned broader principles of public land ownership in the United States" (Linowes et al. 1988, 242).

This attempt at disposal failed because the Reagan administration did not take into account the de facto property rights inherent in our political land system. For example, with more than fifty years of grazing access to federal lands, many ranchers feel their implicit rights to graze on the public domain are threatened by a change of ownership. Many western ranches abut federal land and depend on federal grazing permits for their success. For those ranches the value of the grazing permits has been capitalized into the cost of the deeded land and hence represents a real cost of doing business. Because sales of deeded land include the value of federal leases in the sale price, forcing the owners to buy the grazing leases from the federal government would force them to pay twice. For the same reason, efforts to raise grazing fees have been met by stiff opposition from ranching interests. This opposition generally has been successful despite the powerful environmental lobbies that have worked vigorously to raise grazing fees. Similarly, outfitters who have permits to recreate on political lands pay for these rights when they buy the permits from the original owner; in other words, the value of the recreational access is capitalized into the business. To sell these outfitters the right to access would be forcing them to pay twice. Finally, environmentalist who have fought political battles to establish wilderness lands will feel that they have already paid for the rights to keep those lands free from development. Selling the land to commodity interests will seem to environmental groups like a "taking without due process," and selling the lands to environmental interests will be forcing them to pay twice.

This resistance can be mitigated by "grandfathering" these values in the short term and giving existing "owners" preemption rights. For example, grazing and recreational permit holders could be given their permits to surface use free of charge for ten years with the option to buy the land outright at the end of the period. These arrangements could be made before any disposal process and would be binding on all future landowners. If permittees have purchased their permits with other assets or made any capital investments on their leases, the ten-year grace period would allow them to capture a return on their investment. Where timber sales and subsurface rights to minerals on federal lands have already been parceled out, little change would be necessary except to note that these arrangements would become binding to future landowners as well.

For environmental groups who have already paid for wilderness land through lobbying efforts in the political process, rights (including subsurface mineral and energy rights) to lands already designated as wilderness could be parceled out by lottery to bona fide, bonded environmental groups interested in owning the lands. As owners, it would be up to them to decide whether commodities should be produced on the lands. Because they would get the revenues from such production, they would have an incentive to consider the opportunity cost of not producing.

On lands or minerals where political rights have not be distributed, such as outer continental shelf lands, a simple auction could be used to distribute the resources and receipts could apply toward debt retirement.[11]

Turning to the question of which lands to privatize first, the obvious answer is those lands for which rights have already been allocated. Such rights are fairly clear on those lands where a system of leasing or user fees is in place. These rights could be allocated under preemption as described above.

In the case where political rights have not been assigned, the nomination system used for outer continental shelf lands could be used. Under this system the most valuable tracts are nominated for leasing by interest groups interested in obtaining the lease. A similar system could be applied to onshore federal lands, and noncommodity interests could be encourage to nominate lands. The government could solicit nominations from private parties and auction the lands to the highest bidder.

Although recreational and environmental amenities have not been included in most leasing and user-fee systems for political lands, these amenities can also be privatized for profit or not for profit. Once privatized, there would be an incentive for owners to trade off traditional and nontraditional land uses, charge fees for recreation use, control access, and prevent the overcrowding now so prevalent in national parks. If environmental values remain that cannot be captured by private owners, let the government lease back those aspects as it does with the Conservation Reserve Program on private farmlands.

Conclusion

With 40 percent of the nation's lands under governmental ownership, the United States is one of the more socialistic countries in the world.

Efficiency arguments point toward the benefits of privatization, but there is never a constituency for efficiency. There are, however, constituencies for environmental quality and fiscal responsibility, and it is these constituencies that can be coalesced for privatization. Commenting on the 1988 report of the President's Commission on Privatization, James J. Kilpatrick (1988) said, "Philosophically the proposals are sound. Politically they are extremely difficult. And because politics counts for more than philosophy in Washington, don't hold your breath until the Postal Service goes private. It's a good idea, but its time hasn't come." If privatization is now philosophically sound, we have come a long way since the word was coined in the late 1970s. With more evidence on the perverse results of political land management and the efficacy of private ownership, we can make equal strides toward making privatization of political lands an idea whose time has come.

Notes

1. Throughout this chapter we shall refer to lands controlled by the federal government as political rather than public lands because political land more accurately describes how the land is managed.

2. A bill introduced by Senator Kempthorne (S.1364), under consideration in the Senate, offers property and estate tax incentives to landowners who protect endangered species habitat.

3. For a more detailed discussion of the argument for retention, see Clawson (1983, ch. 4).

4. The percentage is nearly 40 percent if state, county, and local control is included.

5. This cost does not include the overhead costs associated with general administration (e.g., regional and Washington offices).

6. It should be noted, however, that wildlife ranching where thousands of acres are fenced and the wildlife is privately owned works well in South Africa.

7. Based on a survey of five private campgrounds located around Yellowstone National Park, September 1987.

8. This section is based on Leal (1995).

9. State school trust lands are lands that were granted to the state of Montana by the federal government when Montana was admitted to the union. The purpose is to support common schools, state universities, and other institutions.

Of the total trust, 485,000 acres are classified as commercially operable timberlands. In this chapter, we refer to these acres as "state forests."

10. This quotation comes from the Multiple-Use Sustained-Yield Act. See 16 U.S.C. § 531 (a) (1988).

11. For a further discussion of these privatization alternatives in a historical perspective, see Anderson and Hill (1990).

References

Anderson, Terry L. 1992. "Prices, Property Rights, and Profits: Market Approaches to Federal Land Management." In *Multiple Use and Sustained Yield: Changing Philosophies for Federal Land Management?* prepared by the Congressional Research Service, Library of Congress. Committee Print No. 11. Washington, D.C.: U.S. Government Printing Office, December, pp. 173–89.

Anderson, Terry L., and Peter J. Hill. 1990. "The Race for Property Rights." *Journal of Law and Economics* 33 (April): 177–97.

Anderson, Terry L., and Donald R. Leal. 1991. *Free Market Environmentalism.* San Francisco: Pacific Research Institute.

Baden, John, and Richard L. Stroup. 1981. "Saving the Wilderness: A Radical Proposal." *Reason* (July): 29–36.

Barton, Katherine, and Whit Fosburgh. 1986. "The U.S. Forest Service." In *Audubon Wildlife Report.* New York: National Audubon Society.

Blood, Tom, and John Baden. 1984. "Wildlife Habitat and Economic Institutions: Feast or Famine for Hunters and Game." *Western Wildlands* 10(1): 8–13.

Chase, Alston. 1986. *Playing God in Yellowstone: The Destruction of America's First National Park.* Boston/New York: Atlantic Monthly Press.

Clawson, Marion. 1983. *The Federal Lands Revisited.* Washington, D.C.: Resources for the Future.

Coffin, James B., ed. 1996. "FS Gets Entry Fee Powers." *Federal Parks and Recreation* 14(3): 5–6.

Conservation Foundation. 1985. *National Parks for a New Generation: Visions, Realities, Prospects.* Washington, D.C.: Conservation Foundation.

Council on Environmental Quality. 1984. *15th Annual Report of the President's Council on Environmental Quality.* Washington, D.C.: U.S. Government Printing Office.

Donaldson, Thomas. 1970. *The Public Domain.* New York: Johnson Reprint Corporation.

Foldvary, Fred. 1994. *Public Goods and Private Communities: The Market Provision of Social Services.* Brookfield, Vt.: Edward Elgar Publishing Company.

Hardin, Garrett. 1968. "The Tragedy of the Commons." *Science* 162: 1243–48.

Henkel, Mark. 1985. *The Hunter's Guide to Montana.* Helena, Mont.: Falcon Publishing Co.

Kilpatrick, James J. 1988. "Report on Privatization Should Be Taken Seriously." *Greenville News*, March 15.

Leal, Donald R. 1995. *Turning a Profit on Public Forests.* PERC Policy series, PS-4. Bozeman, Mont.: Political Economy Research Center.

Linowes, David F., et al. 1988. *Privatization: Toward More Effective Government.* Report of the President's Commission on Privatization. Urbana and Chicago: University of Illinois Press.

Lueck, Dean. 1983. "The Private Protection of Natural Environments." Master's thesis, University of Montana at Missoula.

Nash, Roderick, ed. 1976. *The American Environment.* Menlo Park, Calif.: Addison-Wesley.

National Wildlife Federation. 1984. "Where the Antelope Roam." In *National Wildlife Federation: Annual Report 1984.* Washington, D.C.: National Wildlife Federation.

O'Toole, Randal. 1988. *Reforming the Forest Service.* Washington, D.C.: Island Press.

———. 1995. "Tarnished Jewels: The Case for Reforming the Park Service." *Different Drummer* 2(1): 27.

Reilly, William K. 1987. Foreword to *American Outdoors: The Legacy, the Challenge,* by President's Commission on Americans Outdoors. Washington, D.C.: Island Press.

Sakolski, A. M. 1932. *The Great American Land Bubble.* New York: Harper and Brothers Publishers.

Taylor, Robert C., Bruce Beattie, and Kerry R. Livengood. 1980. "Public vs. Private Systems for Big Game Hunting." Paper presented at conference, Property Rights and Natural Resources: A New Paradigm For Environmental Movement, the Political Economy Research Center, Bozeman, Montana, December.

U.S. Department of Agriculture. Forest Service. 1994. *Land Areas of the National Forest System,* September 30. Available on-line: www.fs.fed.us.

U.S. Department of the Interior. Bureau of Land Management. 1981. *Public Land Statistics, 1980* Washington, D.C.: U.S. Government Printing Office.

———. 1994. *Public Land Statistics, 1993.* Washington, D.C.: U.S. Government Printing Office.

U.S. Fish and Wildlife Service. Division of Realty. 1995. *Annual Report of Lands under Control of the U.S. Fish and Wildlife Service.* Arlington, Va.: U.S. Government Printing Office. September 30.

U.S. Forest Service. 1980. *An Assessment of the Forest and Range Land Situation in the United States.* Washington, D.C.: U.S. Government Printing Office.

Fixing the
Endangered Species Act

Calculating the Incalculable

What should be done about protecting endangered species? The simple
answer is to fully fund and enforce the Endangered Species Act (ESA).
But the cost of funding and enforcing the ESA as it is currently written
and understood by the courts is potentially infinite. The Supreme Court
declared in its Telleco Dam decision that the act defines "the value of
endangered species as incalculable," that endangered species must "be
afforded the highest of priorities," and that "whatever the cost" species
losses must be stopped (*TVA v. Hill*, 437 U.S. 187, 174, 184 [1978]).
Despite the "incalculable value" of endangered species, federal and state
agencies spent just $171,811,000 on protecting them in 1991; more than
half that amount was spent on just 7 of the 639 species that were on the
endangered species list that year, and 90 percent was spent on 54 species.
The rest were left to fend for themselves (U.S. Fish and Wildlife Service
1992).

The relatively small amount of funding Congress has appropriated
for endangered species programs suggests that Congress is unwilling to
consider the policy implications of legislation the Court interprets as
stating that the worth of endangered species is incalculable. Others have

not been so reticent. Reed Noss (1992, 1994), editor of the scientific journal *Conservation Biology*, argues, for example, that huge amounts of land must be set aside and that, for a species to maintain genetic variation sufficient to cope with environmental uncertainty and to guard against nature's catastrophes, an interbreeding population of at least fifteen hundred to two thouand individuals must be maintained. Thus, Noss claims, 484 million acres are required to support a minimum viable population of two thousand grizzlies, 400 million acres are needed for two thousand wolverines, and 200 million acres for two thousand wolves.[1] By 1995 there were nearly one thousand species on the Endangered Species List, more than three thousand others waiting to be listed (Carroll et al. 1995), and a few thousand more waiting to be "discovered."[2] To save all the habitat that is required to protect minimum viable populations of all these endangered species will require depopulating large areas of the United States.

In fact, Noss (1992, 1994) and others propose that at least half the land area of the forty-eight contiguous states be set aside as nature reserves to protect biodiversity and to save endangered species. Of this total, they recommend that 50 percent be returned to a wilderness state—that is, 25 percent of the lower forty-eight states are to be depopulated and another 25 percent are to be buffer zones (Noss and Cooperrider 1994).

Few Americans will be willing to give up their jobs, cars, and homes or forgo having children in order to preserve 50 percent of the country as nature reserves. Although claiming each species has incalculable value may provide psychic benefits at meetings of the faithful on Earth First! camping trips or at National Wildlife Federation board meetings, this claim provides no policy guidance. It is, in fact, an absurd statement. Few citizens believe that preserving one of the thousands of varieties of beetles is more valuable than solving the economic and social crises of our central cities. But to say that a species must be protected regardless of economic cost assumes that only the "God squad"[3] stands between spending the entire U.S. budget on species preservation versus other pressing problems.

When the ESA was passed in 1973, most members of Congress assumed they were voting to protect charismatic species—grizzlies, whales, manatees, whooping cranes, bald eagles, and the like. The ESA does protect charismatic species, but they are only a tiny portion of all species. Most of the 10 to 100 million species are fungi, insects, bacteria, and plants (Wilson 1992, 32), and the ESA is supposed to protect them all. Thus, incalculable value is assigned to each species whether it is the bald eagle, furbish lousewort, whooping crane, welsh's milkweed, grizzly bear, or tooth cave spider.

When they voted to protect endangered species, lawmakers did not expect that the ESA would be used as a land-use planning tool. If, however, any one of the birds, mammals, plants, insects, fungi, or bacteria located on a person's land is listed as endangered, the ESA controls many of the uses of the land. Restrictions can range from mild irritations to loss of almost all economic value of the land. Because of the ESA, the salt marsh harvest mouse is powerful enough to hold back a bulldozer and the inch-long delta smelt can reduce freshwater pumping for cities and farms. The secretary of the interior, however, is prohibited by law from considering economic effects when deciding to list a species.

The costs the secretary *cannot* consider are considerable. Half the economic activity around Bruneau, Idaho, for example, was threatened when the U.S. Fish and Wildlife Service (FWS) began cutting off water rights to fifty-nine farms and ranches in order to protect the Bruneau Hot Springs snail.[4] In Oregon and Washington, millions of acres of productive timberlands are off-limits for timber harvest as are similar amounts of loblolly pine stands on private and public lands in the South. Western rangelands are subject to use prohibitions because of the desert tortoise and numerous desert plant species, while mining phosphates and other minerals has been banned in much of northern Florida. Property owners in the Texas hill country face criminal prosecution if they clear brush along their fencerows. The Ute and Navajo tribes' water rights are being expropriated by the federal government to protect endangered species. Highways are being rerouted and airport expansions prohibited all across the country. The kangaroo rat regulations in Riverside County, California, effectively make the rat the largest landowner in the county. Current plans to save the Sacramento delta smelt are likely to cost billions.[5] According to Ike Sugg, an analyst at the Competitive Enterprise Institute in Washington, D.C., "conservative estimates of the act's costs are in the tens of billions of dollars" (Sugg 1993, A15).

Proponents of the ESA argue that the act causes minor economic harm. A 1992 World Wildlife Fund (WWF) analysis of 71,560 federal agency consultations from 1987 to 1991, for example, found only eighteen projects that were stopped because they would endanger a species (Barry et al. 1992). Many of the agency consultations, though, were telephone calls to FWS requesting a list of endangered species. Of the two thousand consultations that went on to formal consultations, jeopardy opinions[6] were issued for three hundred and fifty. Eighteen activities were blocked and thirty-five were left unresolved. The WWF study uses these data to show that, depending on the outcomes of the unresolved cases, from 0.9 percent to 2.65 percent of the two thousand formal consultations and 4.1 percent to 15.1 percent of the jeopardy opinions stopped proposed actions.

Looking closely at the WWF numbers, however, produces different conclusions. Of the 350 jeopardy opinions, 169 were separate opinions for a single EPA pesticide program. The percentage of actions blocked rises to as much as 24 percent by considering these 169 opinions as one. The results also change dramatically if the forty-four timber sales adversely affected by the spotted owl decisions are included in the analysis (National Wilderness Institute 1994, 18–19). Moreover, the WWF analysis does not consider the costs of changing or even dropping a project at the first mention of the ESA, the costs of attempting to obtain an incidental take permit, or the costs of delaying projects, often indefinitely.

Another illustration of costs missed by the WWF study is provided by the pocket mouse, a rodent rediscovered in 1993 after not having been seen since 1971. The mice were found during an environmental survey for a resort proposed for 121 acres overlooking Dana Point Harbor, California. The survey found thirty-nine mice on four acres of the site. The U.S. Fish and Wildlife Service moved quickly to place the mouse on the emergency endangered species list, thereby delaying the 400-room hotel complex and 394 homes. The *Los Angeles Times* quoted a spokesman for the local chapter of the Audubon Society as welcoming the listing because, although possibly not stopping the project, the mouse will delay it (Haldane and Hall 1994, B1).

Projects like Dana Point Harbor are being delayed all across the country by the ESA. The U.S. Fish and Wildlife Service's (1993) *Report to Congress* estimates that "approximately 25% of all listed species have conflicts with development projects or other forms of economic activity." A

Table 1   Conflicting Activities and the Number of Recovery Plans
            in Which Each Is Mentioned

Activity	Number of Plans
Agriculture	153
Cattle	100
Collecting	117
Development	245
Grazing	128
Habitat manipulation	199
Hunting/fishing	83
Irrigation	43
Mining	121
Off-road vehicles	63
Outdoor recreation	146
Pesticides	150
Water development	147
Wetlands degradation	21

SOURCE: National Wilderness Institute (1994, 39).

content analysis of 306 recovery plans shows the expected conflicts detailed in table 1. With more than three thousand species as possible
candidates for listing, the amount of economic conflict will expand ex-
ponentially.

Pretending to Protect Species

Leaving aside the equity issue, the costs imposed on private citizens
might be worthwhile if the ESA were actually accomplishing its purposes.
Those purposes, however, are not being met. The ESA authorizes the
FWS to create "critical habitat designations" and requires development
of recovery plans for species on both the threatened and the endangered
lists. The purpose is to identify species in trouble, protect them initially,
and develop plans and programs to restore the populations to viable
levels. During its first twenty years, almost all the activity under the ESA
has been to list species rather than help them recover. As a result, by
1992 the General Accounting Office (GAO) found that critical habitat
was designated for just 16 percent of the species listed and that just 61

percent had a recovery plan in effect (Corn 1995, 2). In addition, twenty species have been delisted, eight because they have gone extinct and eight more because the original data used to justify listing were in error (U.S. Fish and Wildlife Service 1994, 41–42). There is considerable controversy about whether the ESA had any effect on the four species the FWS claims recovered because of the ESA (Competitive Enterprise Institute 1995, 2–3).

The U.S. Fish and Wildlife Service's (1993) *Report to Congress on the Endangered and Threatened Species Recovery Program* claimed to be the "first comprehensive accounting" of conservation and recovery efforts since 1967 and stated that "reclassifications and delistings demonstrate that there can be successes in recovery." The report identified just five delistings, however, and only two, the Rydberg milk vetch and the alligator, are for the continental United States. The alligator would probably not have qualified if today's standards had been applied at the time of listing. The other three delisted species are the Palau owl, dove, and fantail. Palau is a U.S. trust territory hundreds of miles east of the Philippines, and, according to one FWS official, it appears the early counts of these species underestimated their populations. Regardless of the count, their numbers significantly recovered as their habitat recovered after World War II (Gordon 1993, 3).

News releases from environmental groups on the twentieth anniversary of the ESA praised the act for having kept organisms from extinction. Secretary of the Interior Bruce Babbitt (1994, 55) called the act "the most innovative, wide-reaching and successful environmental law that has been passed in the past quarter century." But four contested delistings hardly qualify the ESA for such accolades, especially because for the past decade an average of thirty-eight species a year have been added to the list; of all listed species only 10 percent are improving, and the backlog of species waiting to be listed keeps growing (Reid 1994, 5–6).

Endangered species policy has become an exercise in dishonesty. Species are listed but not recovered, the costs of carrying out the act's public purposes are disproportionately borne by private landowners, and the funding mechanism is not designed to change the situation. Few of the politicians, judges, or bureaucrats who designed, interpreted, and implemented the law intended to be dishonest. They just failed to consider the implications of the rules they put in place. But it is time to stop pretending we are saving species and adopt effective policies. We must understand why the lists of endangered and threatened species keep getting longer in the face of thirty years of legislation. We need to ask why only a few species have ever been taken off the list. And we have to ask where the money will come from to pay for the species currently on the lists as well as each of the thousands waiting to be listed.

Basic Principles

Some insights on how to create a new ESA come from a 1934 essay by Aldo Leopold titled "Conservation Economics" (Flader and Callicott 1991, 193–202). Leopold's insights, as usual, are telling. He begins the essay by noting that the accepted theory of his day about the birth of the moon was that it occurred when a large planet passed near enough to earth to pull off a large piece of the earth into space as a new heavenly body. He compares the birth of conservation programs to that same process:

> Conservation, I think, was "born" in somewhat the same manner in the year A.D. 1933. A mighty force, consisting of pent-up desires and frustrated dreams of two generations of conservationists, passed near the national money-bags whilst opened wide for post-depression relief. Something large and heavy was lifted off and hurled forth into the galaxy of the alphabets. It is still moving too fast for us to be sure how big it is, or what cosmic forces may rein on its career. . . .
>
> [Conservation's] history in America may be compressed into two sentences: We tried to get conservation by buying land, by subsidizing desirable changes in land use, and by passing restrictive laws. The last method largely failed; the other two have produced some small samples of success.
>
> The "New Deal" expenditures are the natural consequence of this experience. Public ownership or subsidy having given us the only taste of conservation we have ever enjoyed, the public money-bags being open, and private land being a drug on the market, we have suddenly decided to buy us a real mouthful, if not indeed, a square meal.
>
> Is this good logic? Will we get a square meal? These are the questions of the hour. (quoted in Flader and Callicott 1991, 193–94)

These continue to be the questions of the hour. To continue Leo-pold's analogy, conservation was hurled into a higher orbit with even greater infusions of government cash and regulations beginning in 1970. To the "galaxy of the alphabets" were added EPA, ESA, CIRCLA, RPA/ NFMA, and hosts of others. The big difference in the years since 1970, as compared with 1933–1970, is that government-sponsored conserva-tion rediscovered an even stronger drug than private land—direct com-mand and control regulation—even though Leopold claimed that that method had largely failed.

It continues to fail today. In fact, as Leopold said in the "Report to the American Game Conference on an American Game Policy" in 1930 (Flader and Callicott 1991, 151), "the present order is radically unsatis-factory; . . . and mild modifications of it will not do." He cautioned against "timidity, optimism, or unbending insistence on old grooves of thought." Today's policymakers would do well to follow his advice.

To develop new "grooves of thought," I propose eight principles, four of them political and four ecological. They are hardly startling or radical but are natural extensions of the lessons since 1933 and, in fact, reaffirm many of the principles promoted by Aldo Leopold as he tried to direct the development of a positive political ecology. If followed, however, existing management systems will be altered dramatically and the ESA will be replaced with pragmatic, effective, intellectually honest policy.

The political principles are

- Conserving habitat and species requires enlisting private property owners on the side of conservation.

- Positive incentives are more effective than penalties if for no other reason than penalties are ex post facto.

- Decentralizing biodiversity activities is more effective than cen-tralizing them. That is, twenty competing answers are better than one, especially because no one knows which one is the right an-swer.

- Depoliticizing biodiversity changes incentives for private individ-uals, public officials, and interest-group representatives and thereby improves the chances of spending funds effectively and creates more private support for conservation.

The biological principles are

- Preserving habitat is a more important and achievable goal than saving all species.
- Global extinctions are more serious than local extinctions, which are more serious than local population extinctions.
- Preventing ecological wrecks is more efficient and possible than rescuing them.
- Managing nature protects biological integrity better than "natural regulation."

These principles lead away from the idealism and moral content of much of the endangered species debate and try to inject pragmatism into the discussion. They permit noble goals while suggesting policies that allow for experimentation and creativity.

There is little chance of these principles being adopted under existing endangered species legislation because they need a more decentralized framework to be effective. If Congress will allow more decentralization and innovation, that is, if politicians, interest groups, and agency personnel will move beyond what Leopold called "unbending insistence on old grooves of thought," there is hope that meaningful, effective policies will emerge.

INCLUDE HABITAT IN THE SPECIES EQUATION

Suzanne Winckler (1992, 74) was correct when she wrote in the *Atlantic Monthly* that "it makes little sense to rescue a handful of near-extinct species. A more effective strategy would focus on protecting eco-systems that support maximum biological diversity." Such an approach would spend money to rescue the whooping crane because there is appropriate and possibly adequate summer and winter habitat and within that habitat are the species on which the crane preys. It would *not* make sense, however, to make heroic efforts to save the California condor in the wild because the requirements of its habitat are likely to never be met again. It also would likely reject efforts to protect the lynx and wolverine in the northern Rockies; they were historically rare *because* the habitat is not well suited to them.

RANKING GLOBAL, LOCAL, AND POPULATION EXTINCTIONS

Because resources are scarce, the nation cannot afford to save every population, every subspecies, or even every species, which means that policymakers will have to make tough choices and rank their priorities. Mann and Plummer (1992, 66) quote Gardner Brown, an economist at the University of Washington, on this issue: "We can't save every species out there, but we can save a lot of them if we want to, and save them in ways that make sense economically and scientifically. To do that, we have to make some choices about which species we are going to preserve. And nobody wants to do that! Nobody!" Mann and Plummer asked if nobody wanted to make choices "because they are dismayed by the prospect of playing God?" Brown responded, "Oh, sure. But in this case God is just sitting on his hands, which is a pretty dangerous thing for him to do."

A nation sitting on its collective hands is dangerous, but that will continue to happen if the legislative mandate continues to be "save everything." A more realistic although less emotionally satisfying rule is to establish priorities and make trade-offs.

PREVENTION VERSUS RESCUE

Almost everyone who writes on endangered species policy calls for earlier conservation efforts than those of the ESA. Under the current process, populations often fall to nearly irreversible lows before being nominated for listing. The biological and ecological problems of trying to recover a species that is nearly gone are immense. The management problems are also intensified when dealing with a species approaching extinction. Clark, Reading, and Clarke (1994, 424–25) explain:

As a species continues to decline and approach extinction, management options narrow, costs rise sharply, and the sense of urgency grows nerve-rackingly high. Fear of failure can become paralyzing; flexibility for experimentation approaches nil. As a result, the context of the recovery program deteriorates into a politically charged and conflict-laden mess with little room for maneuvering. Simply starting conservation *before* a species is severely endangered would alleviate much of the pressure, keep more options open, and reduce the costs.

More options at less cost ought to be the motto of species preservation. Choosing such a path will require tough choices, but it makes little sense to spend large sums of public money on a species or habitat that is nearly gone if the opportunity cost is to let other species slide into a steeper decline.

MANAGING NATURE

Academic ecologists have abandoned "the balance of nature" as a useful tool, but it still underlies most political and lay discussions of conservation. Al Gore's 1992 book, *Earth in the Balance*, for example, worries about the earth's critical, almost spiritual, balance being upset. By contrast, ecologists make statements such as "the classical paradigm in ecology, with its emphasis on the stable state, its suggestion of natural systems as closed and self-regulating, and its resonance with the non-scientific idea of the balance of nature, can no longer serve as an adequate foundation for conservation" (Pickett et al. 1992, 84). The lesson is that there is a strong role for humans in managing the "natural" world because current ecological processes have been structured by human actions, and removing human effects, including fire, will substantially change habitats and processes, not necessarily for the better (Budiansky 1995; Kay 1995). Thus, simply setting lands aside as wilderness or preserves and then letting nature take its course will not save species or protect ecological integrity (Botkin 1990).

ENLISTING PROPERTY OWNERS

The single most important step a new endangered species act should take is to remove the ability of government agencies to, in effect, take 50 percent, 20 percent, or any percentage of someone's property without compensation. A property right is just as important as the right to free speech, to a free press, or to assemble. Speaking at the Smithsonian Earth Day Conference on Biodiversity, Randal O'Toole (1995a, 1) explained the relationship: "Imagine that freedom of the press meant that the government could censor 'only' 20 percent of *U.S. News and World Report* or the *Wall Street Journal.* Or imagine that freedom of assembly meant that the government could forbid 'only' 20 percent of all public or private meetings. Anyone would argue that such freedoms would be meaningless under these conditions." The way in which the U.S. Fish and Wildlife Service sometimes exercises its power under the ESA makes private property just as meaningless. The intellectual justification for making private property rights less meaningful, however, is an economic argument—that the members of the species are not private goods but public goods and their public good nature justifies taking some portion of people's property.

Economists define public goods as those goods for which provision is nonexclusive and consumption is nonrivalrous, and the standard economic assumption is that public goods must be provided by government. Technically, most species are more correctly defined as common pool resources. That is, their provision is nonexclusive but their consumption is rivalrous. There are, however, aspects of endangered species that are public goods: ecological functions, sources of knowledge that can be turned to consumptive and nonconsumptive human uses, sources of scientific information, models, and theory. The benefits flow to everyone, and anyone's consumption of those benefits does not diminish anyone else's consumption. Even aesthetic arguments about endangered species can be thought of in public goods terms; if we allow species loss to continue, each of us is impoverished, or our soul is.

It may be that this public good nature of species in general is why opponents of the Fifth Amendment takings arguments are appalled by notions that people might have to be compensated if government regulators reduce the economic value of private land. Opponents of the argument view the landowner as a polluter who should be either fined for his actions or stopped altogether. After all, landowners are reducing an endowment the earth provides to all (by *all* they mean not just humans but all species). In fact, the arguments are that these landowners are taking an immoral and unfair step. John Humback, a property rights expert at Pace University argues: "The whole idea that government needs to pay people not to do bad things is ridiculous. The reason the government exists in the first place is to define what is for the common good and what's not" (Harbrecht 1994, 6).

A similar objection was voiced by Secretary of the Interior Bruce Babbitt, whose concern was that some groups were using takings arguments to resist protecting endangered species. In one of his speeches he argued against bills such as House Bill 1388, titled the "Just Compensation Act of 1993." (This bill, if passed, would have required federal agencies to compensate property owners "for any diminution in value" caused by environmental regulations.)

> Let's examine the implications of this proposed raid on the public treasury. The Kesterson National Wildlife Refuge in California is one of the great migratory bird stops on the Pacific flyway. But a few years ago, the waterfowl were dying, and they were deformed at birth. It turned out to be selenium poisoning running off into the refuge from nearby farm irrigation wastewater. Under the Endangered Species Act, I tell the farmers: Clean up the pollution or we'll sue you. But under this new proposal, I am undeniably causing a "diminution in value" of a property right—it will cost those farmers money to clean up. They'll comply, but then they'll send me the bill! The old legal maxim, "make the polluter pay," would be replaced by a new legal rule: "it pays to pollute; the government will reimburse your costs." (Babbitt 1994, 55)

Secretary Babbitt's example is indicative of the efforts to mischaracterize property rights arguments and of a fundamental misunderstanding of the nature of property rights and the proper role of government in protecting them.

As any introductory economics textbook explains, one justification of government action is preventing one party from harming others and their properties and, failing that, punishing those who transgress against others in this manner. This is the aim of controlling pollution—controlling the unwanted imposition of wastes or toxins by one party on another. Pollution is a "trespass" or "nuisance" under the principles of common law, and those trespassed against can use the power of government to seek restitution.

Thus, Mr. Babbitt's claim that corporations could profess to be harmed when they are prohibited from injecting toxins into the groundwater simply does not fit within our tradition of property or the evolution of our system of law. Those who pollute are trespassing on others' property and can be stopped without receiving compensation because none is owed them. They are polluters, and the polluter-pays principle demands that the person who pollutes should pay the costs of that pollution.[7] In the Kesterson example the story is complicated by the fact that the selenium-laden water entering the refuge arrived in a publicly funded and managed drainage system built by the Bureau of Reclamation. Without the bureau, the water would never have reached the refuge, so there is some question as to who is the polluter—the farmers or the bureau?

Still, the principle Secretary Babbitt tried to assert is an important one. He wants to establish that reducing habitat or harming an endangered species on private property is pollution—it is an externality landowners are forcing on the rest of the world. Because they are the ones creating costs for others, they should pay to fix the problem. If proponents of this approach can make the externality or pollution argument stick, they will prevail over the constitutional takings argument. If polluters ought to pay *and* if taking an endangered species is pollution, then landowners have fewer rights. They must pay.

Secretary Babbitt's logic is flawed, however, because he does not distinguish between public costs (negative externalities) and public benefits (positive externalities). The pollution-producing landowner passes *costs* on to others who have not contracted to receive them. The biodiversity-producing landowner passes *benefits* on to others who have not contracted for them. The policy responses should be very different—punish those who create costs but reward those who create benefits. But notice that the ESA punishes those who produce benefits. A perverse policy indeed!

But what if property rights are recognized so that a person's property use cannot be reduced without compensation even if a listed species is on the property? If that were the case, landowners would in effect own the species on their property even though the title to the species would rest nominally with the government. The species could then be treated as a private rather than a public good, and those who wish to protect or save the species would operate within markets as opposed to politics as they do now. Instead of property owners being treated as polluters, they would be treated as producers of something others value.

Defenders of Wildlife has already begun to use such methods to protect wolves because it believes that hearing wolves howling again in Montana is a public good (Anderson 1994). Wolves are viewed by ranchers, however, as polluters; that is, wolves kill an occasional cow, calf, or sheep and thereby create uncompensated costs for ranchers. To deal with this wolf "pollution" problem, Defenders of Wildlife offered to pay the ranchers for the costs created by the wolves.

In the spring of 1994, a rancher near Augusta, Montana, collected a $5,000 reward from Defenders for having three wolf pups successfully raised on his property. The rancher told his cowboys to leave the wolves alone following advice from state and federal biologists about how to minimize human disturbance. Without the reward offered by Defenders, many ranchers finding wolves on their property would "shoot, shovel, and shut up."

Defenders of Wildlife have been paying for wolves since 1987, when they created a Wolf Compensation Fund to pay for livestock killed by wolves. So far, the fund has paid $12,000 to about a dozen ranchers. One problem with this approach is that the landowner is not able to decide the price, and although Defenders' compensation insurance program may cover the costs of a replacement cow, it does not pay the rancher for the time spent proving the cow was killed by wolves or arranging for and transporting a replacement cow. It is clearly not a perfect system, but no system is. And because ranchers' normal means of excluding wolves is to quietly kill them, a system that compensates for use—the user-pays principle—increases the chances that wolves will again be heard in the wild.

By adding a reward for allowing wolves to use one's land, Defenders has turned the liability of being the provider of a public good into an asset. The incentives are turned in a new direction. What is more, the payments are relatively small and are paid by private parties, not out of the public treasury.

Another organization pursuing innovative policies is the Delta Waterfowl Foundation, a private, nonprofit organization dedicated to reversing the downward trend in North American duck populations by stopping the loss of habitat. One of the foundations's programs is Adopt-A-Pothole. Funds are raised from contributors all over North America, each of whom receives an aerial photograph of his or her adopted pot-hole, a quarterly report on its status, and an annual estimate of duck production. The farmer receives $7 an acre to maintain pothole habitat and $30 an acre to restore pothole habitat. In addition, farmers are offered production contracts that pay on the basis of actual numbers of ducks produced. The production contracts encourage farmers to improve and protect nesting habitat.

Results have been impressive. After just two years of operation, contributions totaled nearly $1 million from more than one thousand individuals and organizations and eighteen thousand pothole sites were enrolled. Nest density is twice as great for adopted sites as compared with unadopted sites, and nesting success averages 51 percent for adopted sites compared with 10–15 percent for unadopted ones. The program has even developed a special nesting box that protects ducks from predators. Potholes using the device have nesting success rates of 90 percent (Delta Waterfowl 1994).

There is an important distinction, however, between the Defenders of Wildlife wolf program and the Delta Waterfowl program. The wolf is listed under the ESA; thus ranchers who attract it to their property run the risk of having their property regulated by the FWS. None of the mallard, canvasbacks, shovelers, blue-winged teal, green-winged teal, gadwalls, redheads, or pintail nesting in the prairie potholes are endangered. Farmers know they can attract the ducks without having to worry that the value of their property will be reduced because they protect and develop duck habitat. Thus, they are pleased to be paid to attract ducks by improving habitat and changing farming practices. They win and the ducks win. If the threat of ESA regulations were removed from wolves, western ranchers would be far more interested in attracting wolves than they are now.

POSITIVE INCENTIVES

A host of private individuals and groups such as Delta Waterfowl Foundation and Defenders of Wildlife are using positive incentives to promote species and habitat preservation. The ESA, to the contrary, creates perverse incentives that discourage habitat conservation. Public policy, therefore, needs to change, and policymakers must seek positive incentives along the lines of the following recommendations.

Letting Species Pay. Many endangered species can pay their own way if we will let them. South Africa, for example, decided private entrepreneurs offered the best hope for saving several species of endangered vultures—equivalent in size to California condors. Tourists who wish to view and photograph these endangered raptors pay to see them at "vulture restaurants," where carrion is provided for the birds. Local Boy Scouts gain service hours by hammering carrion bones into fragments small enough for the birds to swallow; the bone fragments, a necessary source of protein, were once broken up by hyenas that are now extinct in the vulture's breeding range (Reiger 1993, 14).

In the United States, a broad range of possibilities allows species to pay their own way, from exotic game ranches in Texas to greenhouses producing endangered cacti for the supermarket trade. In 1979, the FWS revised its regulations and allowed commercial foreign trade in American alligators. Successful alligator farming has exploded wild populations, and universities in the South now offer courses in alligator farming. One entrepreneur received permission to farm alligators in a warm springs area in southern Idaho, an area clearly outside the alligators' normal range. The farmer expects to feed them dead cows from nearby dairy farms, thereby solving a disposal problem for the farmers and gaining a free source of food for his alligators.

The Costa Rican government allows rain forests to pay their way through discovery and patenting of genetic resources. It is often argued that great human benefits will occur from species we have not yet studied. One congressional report asked, "Who knows, or can say what potential cures for cancer and other scourges, present or future, may lie locked up in the structures of plants which may yet be undiscovered, much less analyzed." The problem is that in most countries natural genetic resources cannot be patented, thereby removing any incentive for private companies to prospect for them. Costa Rica, however, allowed the Instituto Nacional de Biodiversidad (INBio) to contract with pharmaceutical companies to prospect for and develop indigenous genetic resources. The first agreement was with Merck, a major international firm, for an initial payment of $1 million over two years. In addition, royalty payments will be made to INBio from commercial sales of products developed (Sedjo and Simpson 1995, 175). Because one-quarter of today's cancer drugs were derived from random testing of organisms, the potential for significant royalties exists.

Let me emphasize the *let* in "letting species pay." Many environmentalists are appalled at the commercialization of wildlife, especially of endangered species. Thus, they will not let the species pay their way. The FWS, for example, in 1983 rejected a proposal to allow for the commercial use (turtle soup, meat, and shell products) of captive-bred green sea turtles. The current controversy over the private Grizzly Discovery Center in West Yellowstone, Montana, is another example. The owner wanted to create a park where the public could see grizzly bears. He proposed stocking the park with nuisance bears from Yellowstone and other parks that would otherwise be killed. But the Park Service would not allow him to have any of its nuisance bears. One member of the Greater Yellowstone Coalition, a local environmental group, was quoted in *Newsweek* as saying she would rather see the bears killed than put into the "artificial" habitat of the private park. She refuses to let the bears pay.

Roger Beattie, a New Zealand conservationist, tells of a similar conversation with an official from the Mt. Bruce Endangered Species Unit. The official took Beattie on a tour of the complex, describing each endangered species and its management. When they came to a species of kakariki, the official explained that the female birds were in one aviary and the males in another. Beattie (1994, 6) asked why, prompting the following exchange:

OFFICIAL: We do not want them to breed any more.

ROGER: Do you mean to say that you have birds in an endangered species unit that you are deliberately not breeding?

OFFICIAL: Yes.

ROGER: Why?

OFFICIAL: We do not know what to do with the extra young birds.

ROGER: Have you thought of selling them?

OFFICIAL: Oh no! You couldn't do that!

Selling the extra young birds, however, would let them pay at least part of the costs of preserving the species. It is an approach that worked well for alligators, provides income from the rain forest, and protects South African vultures. It needs to be used more widely.

Decentralization. Decentralization can mean turning responsibility for endangered species over to the states, but it also can mean encouraging private groups and individuals, as well as local, state, and national officials, to be involved in protecting endangered species. Some groups are willing to help species without compensation, which the ESA should allow. One model is the restoration of the peregrine falcon, an accomplishment of Tom Cade at Cornell University and the Peregrine Fund. Using techniques developed by falconers over centuries, he raised birds in captivity and released them to the wild. The birds nested in surprising places—on bridges going in and out of New York and other cities and on urban skyscrapers. One-way glass and TV monitors were installed so that people could watch the falcons nest, raise their young, and devour pigeons. Today there are more pairs of peregrine falcons nesting in New Jersey than at any time since records have been kept.

The wood duck is another example. Early in this century it was expected to follow the passenger pigeon and Carolina parakeet into extinction because its wetland habitat and the dead trees in which it nested were disappearing. But a massive, national, voluntary campaign to build and place artificial nesting boxes reversed the trend. The wood duck is now the second-most common duck species in North America, and wildlife agencies are encouraging hunters to take more of them and fewer of other species. Imagine Audubon Society members, Boy Scouts, hunters, and other interested citizens (the same groups who organized to save the wood duck) approaching owners of timberlands and asking permission to construct spotted owl nesting boxes today. Very few would give permission. Had the ESA been in place when the wood duck was endangered, few landowners would have been willing to allow the nesting boxes and the wood duck would, in all likelihood, be extinct.

Electric companies attract bald eagles to their property because of the wetlands and ponds created by their cooling operations and because the fenced, patrolled property keeps people from disturbing the birds. The problem is that under the ESA the companies become financially responsible for the eagles they inadvertently attract. The ESA does allow for incidental take permits that absolve the companies of some responsibility, but the process for receiving the permits is cumbersome and expensive. If the rules were changed so that the FWS and private organizations could act like Delta Waterfowl officials, electric companies might behave differently; instead of inadvertently attracting eagles, they might actively encourage them. Think of the difference if, instead of being fined when a young eagle on its first flight is killed flying into power lines, the company were rewarded when a young eagle migrated from the company's property. Consider also the other species that could benefit from a company actively seeking to protect an endangered species and its habitat.

Some people are interested in creating preserves on their property and will go to some expense to protect species on their property, including Roger Beattie and his wife on their New Zealand farm. One block of their farm contains a significant stand of native forest that is home to several native bird species as well as nonnative predators. They fenced off twenty hectares of the native forest as a nature preserve using a six-foot-high predator-proof fence that is a combination of deer, rabbit, and bird netting and electric fencing. Inside the fence, they spent two months setting bait stations and traps to rid the preserve of rats, stoats, cats, and dogs.

The Beatties' goals were to reintroduce the eastern buff weka, a rare bird species, onto the preserve. This species is no longer found in Canterbury but was introduced on the Chatham Islands last century and is abundant there. It took longer to get the permits to transport and release the weka on the reserve than it took to eradicate the predators, but in April 1994 the birds were released. Beattie (1994, 7) said, "Conservationists have spent much time and effort deliberating over how they would reintroduce the weka to Canterbury. We just set out and did it. . . . The success of our private reserve shows there is a better option for nature conservation than preying on taxpayers. That success comes from immediate and effective action." The Beatties plan to capitalize on their success by selling information, assistance, and services for predator-proof nature preserves elsewhere.

Another way private groups can get involved in preserving species is to bid for uses of the public lands. Unfortunately, the law often precludes such bidding. On private land, you may buy timber and not cut it down, pay for a grazing right and leave the grass for wildlife, or hold a mineral right but leave the minerals in the ground. If the same system were applied to public lands, anyone could bid on commodity sales and then use the land for conservation purposes instead of extraction. Allowing public land managers to make such sales would introduce a new dynamic to public lands management, as private parties could preserve habitat they think is significant. We might even envision private groups purchasing conservation easements to public lands.

One Idaho environmentalist, Jon Marvel, has attempted to purchase grazing leases on state lands in Idaho. He believes the state lands are overgrazed and hopes to lease the lands and exclude cows. So far he has failed because, although he outbid the ranchers, the ranchers got the Idaho Land Board to reject his bid. The 1995 Idaho legislature even passed a law to make it difficult for a nonrancher to bid on state grazing lands. But Marvel has taken his case to the Idaho Supreme Court and expects to win. He points to an Oklahoma case in which the court, relying on trust language in the state constitution, ruled that the state could not offer leases to ranchers at below-market rates. Expired Oklahoma leases are now advertised on television (Stuebner 1995, 57). Once the political power of traditional users is broken through court decisions or by increased public attention, whole new patterns of use will emerge, including easements and purchases to protect endangered species.

Under such a system groups that are currently strong opponents of grazing might even use grazing as a management option to benefit endangered species. For example, many private and public wildlife refuges manage vegetation by grazing cows. Research by Charles Kay (1994) at the Idaho Sheep Station concludes that domestic livestock are not necessarily harmful; he found the sheep station's riparian communities to be in excellent condition. What is harmful is a system of political management that does not allow for creativity and adaptation.

DEPOLITICIZING BIODIVERSITY

Enlisting property owners, providing positive incentives, and decentralizing biodiversity protection cannot happen until the process is depoliticized. In part because of the need to continue to generate political support for endangered species protection, the U.S. Fish and Wildlife Service spends most of its money on charismatic species (Dwyer et al. 1995, 738–39). In addition, managers pursue strategies that make little ecological sense but a lot of political sense. The core of a strategy for depoliticizing the process is the budget. Simply put, FWS must pay its way.

The funding mechanism for endangered species protection must be changed in order to carry out this proposal. Currently, the FWS receives a budget from Congress but in reality has almost an unlimited budget in that it can list species and thereby control private landowners' actions without having to pay the costs associated with the listing. If, however, the FWS cannot "take" property without compensation, it will have to make tough choices, especially if it has a fixed budget.

Saying the FWS will have to make tough choices does not imply that biodiversity will be unprotected, just that the mix of policies will change and that managers will have an incentive to innovate. As Richard Stroup, an economist with the Political Economy Research Center, notes, bureaucrats must make choices in order to spur the search for alternative policies. He showed how aluminum can manufacturers reduced the amount of aluminum in each can by more than 60 percent. He suggests bureaucrats will search for the same kinds of efficiencies as they pursue a mandate to maximize biological integrity given a fixed budget.

One proposal for the source of the endangered species budget and for further depoliticizing the process is a biodiversity trust fund that collects a fixed share of public land user fees each year (O'Toole 1995b, 3). A user fee of $6 a day would generate about $4.6 billion a year in addition to the commodity user fees of roughly $3.4 billion. A biodiversity trust fund that received just 10 percent of these fees would have $800 million as compared with the 1994 FWS endangered species appropriation of $6.7 million (Corn 1995, 8). Another possible funding source was suggested by a former Department of the Interior economist, who proposed earmarking a portion of royalty and bonus payments from developing the oil reserves on the Arctic National Wildlife Reserve (Nelson 1995, 122).

A trust fund charged with promoting biodiversity and funded from user fees would relieve many political pressures, as it would replace the system of funding that is based on congressional whim and pork barrel politics. Because the trust's income would be based on fees from federal lands, trustees would have an incentive to make sure the federal land agencies are charging market value for their consumptive and nonconsumptive resources. They would also have a vested interest in informing Congress when resources are being provided at less than their value. O'Toole (1995a, 2) suggests having the biodiversity trust fund managed by a board of trustees made up of conservation biologists and ecologists appointed by cabinet officials such as the secretaries of agriculture and the interior or the director of the Smithsonian Institution and serving nine-year terms. The model for establishing the board of trustees is the Federal Reserve Board. Expenditures from the trust fund would have to be justified before the trustees, who could also accept proposals from state agencies and private groups for protecting biodiversity. Competition for funds would thereby spur innovation and creativity. It would also mean that proposals to spend millions to restore wolves to Yellowstone would compete with proposals to spend the same amount of money to protect a host of truly endangered species across the nation.

Trustees may discover that it makes sense to allow many species into markets where owners have an incentive to protect them. Fee hunting, farming, and captive breeding are all market activities that require relatively few funds to oversee and monitor. Many species that cannot be privatized could still be treated as toll goods. Protecting these species requires trustees to examine a range of positive incentives, from awards or other forms of recognition to cash awards to rental of habitat. The innovative conservation officer will act like Delta Waterfowl and pay for output such as hatchlings per pothole, rather than just habitat set aside.

In those cases where none of these policies can work, that is, where protection *is* a public good, it will make sense to rent or purchase habitat. Even in this case, however, it may not require actually buying the land but buying easements. Landowners might be invited to enroll their lands in a program that required them to manage those lands in a particular way, in return for which they would receive payment or other forms of compensation. In concept the above program resembles the "conservation reserve" or "wetlands reserve" programs of the federal government in that landowners enrolling in those programs commit to certain land management practices and receive payment. Bureaucrats with fixed budgets and a broad range of possibilities for preserving habitat might tie compensation to actual output or attraction of particular species, rather than simply nominally adopting certain management practices, as is the case under the conservation and wetland reserve programs.

The underlying dynamic is that agency personnel or trust fund officers would have a clearly defined mandate and would have to compete for a budget. Thus, there will be strong incentive to innovate and rank choices about species on which to concentrate and about policies that would best meet the conservation objectives. They will have to ask if a particular species or habitat can be protected most efficiently by being treated as a private, public, or toll good. Thus, endangered species policy becomes dynamic, innovative, and purposeful.

Consider landowners whose property harbors kangaroo rats. If Californians in the kangaroo rat study area were offered a reward of $1,900 an acre for land that harbored kangaroo rats instead of being told they could not use land inhabited by rats, they might have a very different view of those who want to protect endangered species and of the kangaroo rat.

The same system could be used for spotted owls and desert tortoises. On a regular basis, a census could be done to determine how many owls or tortoises were on a person's land. A payment would be made for having maintained the population, or an additional reward could be offered for having attracted new owls or turtles. In this way, the owls and turtles become almost the private property of the landowners. The endangered species generate income rather than expenses. By protecting the species and their habitat, the landowners make themselves better off. Such a system could work for a broad range of animal and plant species.

It is impossible to estimate how much money is "needed" to protect endangered species. In fact, need statements make little sense without asking, "at what price?" Given scarce resources we must recognize that, although all species may be important, some are more important than others. Thus, the amount of endangered species protection we "need" depends on the price of providing that protection. If inexpensive ways are found to protect species, more will be protected. Decentralizing species protection provides ways to discover efficiencies and, therefore, protect more species. But until the endangered species budget is fixed and the power to shift costs to others is taken away, the search for innovation and efficiencies will be stifled.

STOP SUBSIDIZING ECOSYSTEM DISRUPTION
ON PRIVATE LANDS

As part of a move to depoliticize and decentralize conservation, federal and state subsidies to private landowners must be ended. Leopold (Flader and Callicott 1991, 199) wrote of laws and programs that "frequently clash, or at best, fail to dovetail with each other." Today subsidies for uses of private lands do not mesh with endangered species protection and often work against it (Losos et al. 1995). The Washington, D.C., promoters of these programs seldom see how they encourage development on fragile lands that would otherwise never be economically feasible to develop. O'Toole (1995a, 1) claims that "more than half of all listed species are largely or primarily threatened by government subsidized activities." These subsidies include everything from below-cost timber sales to animal damage control programs to import tariffs that encourage sugar production near the Everglades.

Loan guarantees and loans at below-market rates of interest have serious ecological consequences. A major conference center is being built in a canyon near my home using loans subsidized by the nation's taxpayers. The development may have eventually occurred without the loans, but the loans are a factor in the development happening now. Similarly, federal crop insurance, flood insurance, and disaster relief all contribute to overdevelopment of private lands.[8]

Ending these subsidies will not stop disruption of all remaining habitats but will stop some, as developers, farmers, and home owners face more of the costs of their own actions. It is no secret that as individuals are made less responsible for their actions their behavior becomes more reckless. Removing subsidies reduces the recklessness.

CHARGE USER FEES ON PUBLIC LANDS

Use of public lands or, more accurately, political lands is determined by political processes that are subject to interest-group pressures, pork barrel politics, and bureaucratic mismanagement. Sally Fairfax, in her foreword to Robert Nelson's book *Public Lands and Private Rights: The Failure of Scientific Management*, says of these lands, "Almost everything we have tried to accomplish on the public lands—from original, eighteenth century efforts to sell the lands and use the receipts to retire the Revolutionary War debt, to current efforts to charge equitable and efficient grazing fees—has failed" (Nelson 1995, xi). One cost of that failure is the destruction of habitat for endangered species. The potential for habitat destruction on political lands is large given that the federal government owns 28 percent of the nation's onshore lands (U.S. Department of the Interior 1993, 5). Those habitats, however, are unnecessarily disrupted by private users who do not pay the costs of their use. More than half of Forest Service timber sales, for example are below-cost sales. Most recreation opportunities are simply given away. Irrigation and municipal water that flow from national forests are worth billions of dollars, yet the national forests receive no income for the water they produce (O'Toole 1988, 12–13). Few users have a direct incentive to protect habitat or species on the political lands, and many have incentives to overuse the lands. Changing incentives for public land users is a major political problem that will require structural changes to the administering agencies—changes like the funding changes I propose for the ESA. Depoliticizing the political lands is indeed a daunting challenge.

Mill Creek Canyon, east of Salt Lake City, Utah, shows how user fees can protect habitat. The canyon was experiencing phenomenal use rates but receiving just $3,000 a year from the Forest Service to manage the human use. Because the area was being trashed, Salt Lake County built a tollbooth just outside the canyon to collect a modest toll from all who enter. The tollbooth is now generating more than $125,000 a year. The county gives the money to the local Forest Service Office under condition it be spent on the canyon for riparian restoration, control and disposal of human and pet waste, and protection of the canyon's fragile watershed (Smart 1994). The same approach can be used in areas of endangered species habitat.

Conclusion

In 1990, Fedelis Lungu, an alumnus of Utah State University's (USU's) College of Natural Resources, returned from Zambia and stopped by my office for a visit. He told how, after receiving his master's degree, he had

returned to his home in Zambia to pursue a career in wildlife management. Lungu soon discovered that managing wildlife meant managing
people because growing human populations were increasingly encroach-
ing into habitat previously used primarily by wildlife. In this setting, he
had to deal with a serious form of human/wildlife conflict—poaching.

Poaching, he found, was rampant in Zambia when he returned. During the 1980s some estimated that as many as 100,000 elephants were
poached in Zambia's Luangua Valley (Ivory Trade Review Group 1989).
Lungu diligently pursued the poachers, and his department finally
caught a fairly major poacher and several village accomplices. The day
they took the case to court was a turning point for him in trying to
protect animals from humans:

> The prosecutor brought the peasants before the court and asked why they
> had helped the poacher. One said, "Because he gave me some trousers,"
> and the other said, "Because he gave me some sugar." Their responses hit
> me like a two-by-four between the eyes. Those of us in the wildlife depart-
> ment were making the peasants' lives worse and the poacher was making
> them better.

Because others learned the same lesson, Zambian officials changed
how they managed people and wildlife. They started to find ways for the
local villagers to benefit from the wildlife, principally by organizing safari
companies the villagers could participate in and benefit from. The income was good enough that the person long suspected of being the
leading poacher in the Luangua Valley began driving a two-ton truck for
Malambo Safari. And instead of chasing poachers, Lungu was in the
United States recruiting customers for Zambia's safari companies.

Peasants will conserve wildlife only if it is in their interest to do so.
Unfortunately for endangered species, the message is the same: people
will conserve species if it is in their interest to do so. Public and private
land managers pursue private agendas that may or may not be in the
public interest. Thus, National Park Service personnel proceed with
their agenda regardless of what the data tell them. Agents of the FWS,
anxious to continue congressional funding, spend most of the endangered species budget on charismatic species like wolves and grizzly bears
and little to aid truly endangered species with less emotional appeal.

Private timber owners accelerate harvesting if they fear their land harbors endangered red-cockaded woodpeckers. Alternatively, they may cut down trees with holes in them, cut them into sections, and dispose of the section with the hole. All cavity nesters lose, including other species of woodpeckers, flickers, screech owls, and flying squirrels.

Positive incentives would cause owners, land users, activists, and policymakers to recognize the costs of their actions and bring human management to the fore. Adopting the proposals presented here would produce multiple approaches to habitat and species preservation instead of the limited policies we have under the ESA. Specifically, government can

- Let species pay their way by allowing private groups and individuals to profit from protecting species and allowing public agencies to charge user fees.

- Decentralize biodiversity protection efforts to states and private organizations. Many competing answers are better than one, especially because no one knows which is the right answer.

- Depoliticize the protection process by creating a biodiversity trust fund that will change incentives for private individuals, public officials, and interest-group representatives and thereby improve the chances of spending funds effectively while creating private support for conservation.

- Stop subsidizing ecosystem disruption on private lands in order to reduce development on fragile lands.

- Charge user fees on public lands so users participate in the costs of preservation as well as pay the costs of their own actions.

The critical question about endangered species policy is, *what decision process is best?* These proposals will not save all species or even keep people from making mistakes. They will result in actions that rely on trial and error, learning from mistakes, and using new knowledge to respond to new challenges and problems. This approach is, therefore, emphatically not a set of "solutions." Instead, it allows us to be resilient in a dynamic, changing world. It harnesses the creativity of people everywhere to innovate, experiment, take new risks, and produce new knowledge; it is, in fact, adaptive management (Walters 1986). Such a process will produce responses we cannot predict from the beginning. Just as those who predicted timber shortages could not foresee chipboard and particleboard or the technology that turned previously valueless trees into usable building materials, thereby creating timber surpluses, this system cannot foresee exact responses to many present and certainly not future species controversies. The best hope is that policymakers will put processes in place that will allow innovation and experimentation to produce those responses.

Aldo Leopold's conclusion to his 1933 essay, "Conservation Economics" (quoted in Flader and Callicott 1991, 202), applies equally well here:

> This paper forecasts that conservation will ultimately boil down to rewarding the private landowner who conserves the public interest. It asserts the new premise that if he fails to do so, his neighbors must ultimately pay the bill. It pleads that our jurists and economists anticipate the need for workable vehicles to carry that reward. It challenges the efficacy of single-track laws, and the economy of buying wrecks instead of preventing them. It advances all these things, not with any illusion that they are truth, but out of a profound conviction that the public is at last ready to do something about the land problem, and that we are offering it twenty competing answers instead of one. Perhaps the cerebration induced by a blanket challenge may still enable us to grasp our opportunity.

Notes

1. Other estimates are somewhat smaller. Bader (1992), for instance, estimated that a minimum of 32 million acres are required to support a population of two thousand grizzly bears. But even this lower estimate represents an area equal to one-third of Montana, the third-largest state in the lower forty-eight.

2. One estimate put the number of plants and animals biologically threatened in the United States at nine thousand (Halverson 1995).

3. The God squad, so named because it is authorized to play God in determining if a species can be allowed to go extinct, included the secretaries of agriculture, army, and the interior, the chairman of the Council of Economic Advisers, the administrators of the Environmental Protection Agency and the National Oceanic and Atmospheric Administration, and an individual to represent the affected state. Five members must vote in favor for an exemption to allowed.

4. See Anderson (1994, 18). A federal judge threw out the listing of the snail under the ESA, citing inadequate data, and stopped the FWS from reducing the flows of water.

5. See Mann and Plummer (1995) and Easterbrook (1995) for extended discussions of economic conflicts.

6. If the FWS or National Marine Fisheries Service finds that a proposed action will jeopardize or adversely modify an endangered species' critical habitat, the agency issues a jeopardy opinion that suggests reasonable and prudent alternative actions. "Reasonable and prudent" are defined by the agency, not by the landowner.

7. The polluter-pays principle addresses the major economic concerns of environmentalism—negative externalities. Negative externalities are costs of one person's actions that are passed on to others without their consent. Water pollution from pesticide residues is an example.

8. For an extended discussion of the environmental consequences of agricultural support programs, see Gardner (1995).

References

Anderson, Terry L. 1994. "Home on the Range for Wolves." *Christian Science Monitor,* April 14, p. 18.

Babbitt, Bruce. 1994. "The Triumph of the Blind Texas Salamander and Other Tales from the Endangered Species Act." *E Magazine* 5(2): 54–55.

Bader, Michael. 1992. "A Northern Rockies Proposal for Congress." *Wild Earth,* special issue, pp. 61–64.

Barry, Dwight J., et al. 1992. *For Conserving Listed Species, Talk Is Cheaper Than We Think.* Washington, D.C.: World Wildlife Fund.

Beattie, Roger. 1994. "Free Market Conservation: Protecting Native Plants and Birds to Death." *The Free Radical,* August, pp. 6–7.

Botkin, Daniel B. 1990. *Discordant Harmonies: A New Ecology for the Twenty-first Century.* New York: Oxford University Press.

Budiansky, Stephen. 1995. *Nature's Keepers: The New Science of Nature Management.* New York: Free Press.

Carroll, Ronald, et al. 1995. *Strengthening the Use of Science in Achieving the Goals of the Endangered Species Act: An Assessment by the Ecological Society of America.* Washington, D.C.: Ecological Society of America.

Clark, Tim W., Richard P. Reading, and Alice L. Clarke. 1994. *Endangered Species Recovery: Finding the Lessons, Improving the Process.* Washington, D.C.: Island Press.

Competitive Enterprise Institute. 1995. *Delisted Endangered and Threatened Species.* Washington, D.C.: Competitive Enterprise Institute.

Corn, Lynne M. 1995. "Endangered Species: Continuing Controversy." *Congressional Research Service Issue Brief* IB95003.

Delta Waterfowl. 1994. *Delta Waterfowl Report.* Deerfield, Ill.: Delta Waterfowl.

Dwyer, Lynne E., Dennis D. Murphy, and Paul R. Ehrlich. 1995. "Property Rights Case Law and the Challenge to the Endangered Species Act." *Conservation Biology* 9: 725–41.

Easterbrook, Gregg. 1995. *A Moment on the Earth: The Coming Age of Environmental Optimism.* New York: Viking.

Flader, Susan L., and J. Baird Callicott, eds. 1991. *The River of the Mother of God: And Other Essays by Aldo Leopold.* Madison: University of Wisconsin Press.

Gardner, B. Delworth. 1995. *Plowing Ground in Washington: The Political Economy of U.S. Agriculture.* San Francisco: Pacific Research Institute.

Gordon, Robert E. 1993. *The Art of Statistics: Fish and Wildlife's Report to Congress on the Endangered and Threatened Species Recovery Program.* Washington, D.C.: National Wilderness Institute.

Haldane, David, and Len Hall. 1994. "Pocket Mouse Added to Endangered Species List, Putting Resort on Hold." *Los Angeles Times*, February 2, p. B1.

Halverson, Anders. 1995. "A Full-Court Press to Save Ecosystems." *High Country News* 27(9): 9–10.

Harbrecht, Doug. 1994. "A Question of Property Rights and Wrongs." *National Wildlife* 32(6): 4–11.

Ivory Trade Review Group. 1989. *The Ivory Trade and the Future of the African Elephant.* Vol. 1. *Summary and Conclusions.* Oxford, Eng.: International Development Centre.

Kay, Charles E. 1994. "An Evaluation of Willow Communities on the U.S. Sheep Experiment Station's Centennial Mountains Summer Range." Unpublished report on file, U.S. Sheep Experiment Station, Dubois, Idaho.

———. 1995. "Aboriginal Overkill and Native Burning: Implications for Modern Ecosystem Management." *Western Journal of Applied Forestry* 10: 121–26.

Losos, Elizabeth, Justin Hayes, Ali Phillips, David Wilcove, and Carolyn Alkire. 1995. "Taxpayer-Subsidized Resource Extraction Harms Species." *Bioscience* 45: 446–55.

Mann, Charles C., and Mark L. Plummer. 1992. "The Butterfly Problem." *Atlantic Monthly*, January, pp. 47–70.

———. 1995. *Noah's Choice: The Future of Endangered Species.* New York: Alfred A. Knopf.

National Wilderness Institute. 1994. "Costs of ESA." *NWI Resource* 5(1): 32–39.

Nelson, Robert H. 1995. *Public Lands and Private Rights: The Failure of Scientific Management.* Lanham, Md.: Rowman and Littlefield Publishers.

Noss, Reed F. 1992. "The Wildlands Project: Land Conservation Strategy." *Wild Earth,* special issue, pp. 10–25.

———. 1994. "Building a Wilderness Recovery Network." *The George Wright Forum* 11(4): 17–40.

Noss, Reed F., and Allen Y. Cooperrider. 1994. *Saving Nature's Legacy: Protecting and Restoring Biodiversity.* Washington, D.C.: Island Press.

O'Toole, Randal. 1988. *Reforming the Forest Service.* Washington, D.C.: Island Press.

———. 1995a. *Incentives and Biodiversity.* Available on-line: http://www.teleport.com/~rot/biodiver.html.

———. 1995b. *Fixing the Endangered Species Act.* Available on-line: http://www.teleport.com/~rot/esa.html.

Pickett, Steward T. A., V. Thomas Parker, and Peggy L. Fiedler. 1992. "The New Paradigm in Ecology: Implications for Conservation Biology above the Species Level." In *Conservation Biology: The Theory and Practice of Nature Conservation, Preservation, and Management,* ed. Peggy L. Fiedler and Subodh Kumar Jain. New York: Chapman and Hall.

Reid, Walter. 1994. "Status and Trends of U.S. Biodiversity." *Different Drummer* 1(3): 5–6.

Reiger, George. 1993. "Footing the Bill." *Field and Stream* 98 (May): 14–18.

Sedjo, Roger A., and R. David Simpson. 1995. "Property Rights Contracting and the Commercialization of Biodiversity." In *Wildlife in the Marketplace,* ed. Terry L. Anderson and Peter J. Hill. Lanham, Md.: Rowman and Littlefield Publishers.

Smart, Angela. 1994. "Recreational User Fees on Public Lands." Master's thesis, Utah State University at Logan.

Stuebner, Stephen. 1995. "Bidding War for State Rangelands." *Different Drummer* 2(3): 57.

Sugg, Ike. 1993. "If a Grizzly Attacks, Drop Your Gun." *Wall Street Journal,* November 13, pp. A15–16.

U.S. Department of the Interior. Bureau of Land Management. 1993. *Public Land Statistics, 1992.* Washington, D.C.: U.S. Government Printing Office.

U.S. Fish and Wildlife Service. 1992. *Federal and State Endangered Species Expenditures, Fiscal Year 1991.* Washington, D.C.: U.S. Government Printing Office.

———. 1993. *Report to Congress on the Endangered and Threatened Species Recovery Program.* Washington, D.C.: U.S. Government Printing Office.

———. 1994. *Endangered and Threatened Wildlife and Plants.* Washington, D.C.: U.S. Government Printing Office.

Walters, Carl J. 1986. *Adaptive Management of Renewable Resources.* New York: Macmillan.

Wilson, Edward O. 1992. *The Diversity of Life.* Cambridge, Mass.: Belknap Press of Harvard University Press.

Winckler, Suzanne. 1992. "Stopgap Measures." *Atlantic Monthly* 269 (January): 74–78.

Superfund:
The Shortcut That Failed

Superfund has been a disaster.
—President Bill Clinton[1]

Love Canal—the Beginning

Nearly twenty years ago, home owners around Love Canal, an abandoned
waste site in Niagara Falls, New York, found chemicals leaking into their
homes. Crude health studies suggested that the chemicals might have
caused serious diseases and genetic problems. The state of New York
declared a public health emergency. Soon, Love Canal, "toxic waste,"
and "ticking time bombs" became household words.

Ultimately, the entire neighborhood was abandoned, by government decree. Two hundred and thirty-seven homes were bulldozed,
along with a school (see Danzo 1988, 11). Ironically, no scientifically

This chapter is based on a Political Economy Research Center (PERC) Policy
series paper of the same title, drawn from a forthcoming book on Superfund by
Richard L. Stroup and Sandra L. Goodman. Copyright © 1995, PERC. Reprinted
with permission.

credible evidence has ever shown that the health of residents was harmed by the chemical exposure or that the massive disruption, relocation, and cleanup prevented any serious health problems (see Wildavsky 1995).

Although the Love Canal episode has largely ended for those residents, it has left a legacy that affects all Americans. That legacy is Superfund, a government program passed by Congress in 1980 to deal with similar waste sites. The Love Canal situation stimulated passage of the Comprehensive Environmental Response Compensation and Liability Act (CERCLA), the law creating Superfund.

The Superfund Program: Plagued with Problems

Superfund was supposed to be a short, swift program to cleanse the nation of dangerous hazardous waste sites like Love Canal. It was to cost at most a few billion dollars and to be paid for mainly by those whose pollution caused serious harms or risks.

But after fifteen years of activity, cleanup is still slow. High costs and litigation plague the program. By June 1996, 102 sites had been cleaned up, but 1,227 sites remained.[2] The EPA reports that it cost more than $30 million to clean[3] up the sites. In 1992, the EPA reported that its overhead costs in 1988 were more than $328 for every hour of work performed by an individual, normally a contractor's employee, in cleaning up a site. (That is $412 in 1994 dollars.) This does not include the wage or the overhead cost charged by the contractor.[4] According to the Rand Corporation, legal and other transaction costs accounted for 32 percent of total expenditures (Dixon, Drezner, and Hammit 1993, 45).

Many people touched by the program are harmed, including those it is supposed to help. Designation as a Superfund site causes property values to fall. Residents may be forced to move away, at least temporarily. People may be badly frightened for no good reason. The firms required to pay for the cleanups have little chance to defend themselves against being billed enormous sums, and the EPA does not even have to prove that there is a health risk from the site but only that its own decisions were not arbitrary or capricious. Investors and banks often refuse to lend money for development of Superfund sites or sites that might have Superfund liability attached to them. They reject these "brown fields" for untouched "green fields" in the suburbs, far from the inner-city people who need jobs and often beyond the boundaries of cities that need a tax base. Even EPA administrator Carol Browner, supervisor of the program in the Clinton administration, has criticized the program as one that "frequently moves too slowly, cleans up too little, has an unfair liability scheme and costs too much" (quoted in Prestley 1995, 58).

The purpose of this chapter is to assess what went wrong with Superfund and to recommend ways to solve the problems. In doing so, I hope also to shed light on the problems that affect other programs that the Environmental Protection Agency administers to reduce pollution.

Congress Rejects the Past

The strongest complaints about Superfund have been that few sites have been cleaned up, too much is spent on lawyers and administrative costs, and cleanups are too costly. (See the quotations in the appendix.) These are legitimate complaints, but problems of this sort with government programs are not unusual. Such programs are rarely labeled "a disaster" by the president. Why is Superfund different?

Superfund is different because it has released EPA and Superfund managers from the restraints that hold back most government programs. The EPA can spend potentially unlimited sums of money on cleaning up sites, without having to back its decision with evidence of serious harm or risk. The EPA must follow procedures such as notifying potentially responsible parties of its actions and accepting public comment. But there is no impartial review of EPA decisions. Courts can decide only whether officials are following these procedures and whether they have been arbitrary or capricious. In addition, three special taxes raise money earmarked for Superfund. Superfund is not restrained by the checks and balances that normally characterize government.

Superfund was enacted in an atmosphere of crisis. The rights of the people living near Love Canal had been violated. But Congress never examined who was actually at fault—who had allowed the release of chemicals to occur, what the health risks really were, what the remedy should be, or who should pay for it. Indeed, the supposed perpetrator, Hooker Chemical Company, had acted responsibly. But this was not widely known until several years later and even today is largely ignored in retrospective commentaries on Love Canal (see Zuesse 1981). Hooker's parent company, Occidental Chemical Corporation, paid $129 million for the cleanup and relocation costs.

The people of Love Canal, like others exposed to hazardous waste, had remedies available. The traditional way of dealing with such harm was to go to court under common law to force the owner of the site to clean it and to pay for damages already done. Lawsuits over environmental damage were on record across the nation, and orders from judges to pay damages and stop harmful behavior were not uncommon.

In the tumult of publicity and pressure, however, this history was rejected. One reason was a growing dissatisfaction with the common-law approach. Critics claimed that common law could not deal with hazardous wastes for the following reasons:[5]

- *Lack of proof.* Judges and juries tended to deny relief where the damage was "speculative" or "uncertain." They had to be convinced that a serious harm, or risk of harm, existed and that it had been caused by the action that was to be stopped or the contamination to be remedied. Suspicion and accusations were not enough.

- *Lack of consistency.* Different courts, acting in different jurisdictions or at different times, would not always provide consistent decisions.

- *Lack of public protection.* Private common-law litigation was primarily aimed at protecting individuals or specific groups, not the general public, from specific pollution problems.

- *High costs.* Lawsuits were expensive.

- *Complexity of issues.* In technically complex cases, some judges preferred to transfer the problem to state and federal agencies.

Given these limitations, many people had concluded that the courts could not address illnesses such as cancer, which could be triggered at one point in time but not actually appear until many years later. And the link between chemical exposures and disease might be "probabilistic" rather than clear. Each of these complaints had some basis in fact. Common law was clearly imperfect.

Another factor propelling congressional action was fear that the person who created a dangerous site might not be found or might be insolvent. Love Canal was clearly owned by the city of Niagara Falls. Hooker Chemical, which had put wastes inside the canal, had turned over the deed to the local school board in 1953. In 1960 the school board deeded the land to the city. But the idea that Hooker had somehow "abandoned" the site remained an integral part of the Love Canal story, fueling pressure to do something about "abandoned" or "orphan" sites.

The residents of Love Canal, and their supporters, were in no mood for lengthy court proceedings. They had "scientific" evidence suggesting causal connections between the chemicals and serious health maladies. This evidence was seriously flawed (Wildavsky 1995); it did not show a causal link between the harms and the chemicals. But residents believed it did. New York State health commissioner Robert Whelan, in August 1978, declared a "public health emergency" (although he did so in order to qualify the area for more state funds). In September he issued a report entitled "Love Canal: Public Health Time Bomb" (Landy, Roberts, and Thomas 1990, 134). New York congressman Jack Kemp referred to toxic wastes as "among the deadliest of silent killers in this country."[6]

Congress pulled out all the stops. It had a ready villain—corporate polluters—to attack, and speed was to be the order of the day. The fine points of legal proof would not stand in the way of saving lives. As the United States Court of Appeals for the Fifth Circuit later said, "Shooting first and asking questions later was the intent of Congress."[7]

CERCLA,[8] the law that resulted from this imbroglio, created a $1.6 billion fund to clean up existing sites over a five-year period. The fund was financed primarily by taxes on the oil and chemical industries, rather than congressional appropriations from general revenues. The law placed liability for the cost of cleanup on those who had some connection to the contaminated site. Companies that produced waste that ended up in the site could be liable for cleanup even if they had not placed contaminants at the site, their actions had not been illegal when they occurred, and no actual harm or clear evidence of serious risk to people in the vicinity was present.

The law exempted the EPA from judicial oversight except at a few points in the Superfund process. Even at those points, those accused (the "potentially responsible parties," or PRPs) could reduce their financial burden only if they could prove that EPA decisions had been arbitrary or capricious.

The law also included a plan for short-term emergency removals of waste to avert an apparent and immediate danger. These were limited to one year in duration and $1 million in cost (later increased to $2 million), although more than one removal action can be ordered at a site. This portion of the Superfund program is relatively small and typically receives little attention, yet it may remove most of the danger actually present at a site. In fact, it is often praised by outside observers (see Wildavsky 1995, 182).

The grand achievement envisioned for Superfund did not materialize. Five years after the law was passed, many of the initially listed sites were still in limbo and a large backlog of additional sites was building up. So the Superfund Amendments and Reauthorization Act (SARA) was passed in 1986. It authorized an additional $8.5 billion in special industry taxes and attempted to streamline the Superfund process by narrowing the discretion of EPA's leadership. For example, SARA requires stringent drinking water standards to be applied as cleanup standards, even when the water is not expected to be drunk. And Congress strengthened the provisions that made it difficult to obtain judicial review of the EPA's decisions.[9]

Not Incompetence but Poor Choices

When government programs run into trouble, as Superfund has, observers are quick to assume that incompetent or wrongheaded people are the cause. Some critics blamed the Reagan administration because the Superfund law had been passed by a lame-duck Congress at the end of the Carter administration, and Congress had delegated to the EPA many difficult decisions, such as how sites would be chosen, how risks would be assessed, and how thorough cleanups should be. Because the Reagan administration, rhetorically at least, was committed to deregulation, Superfund supporters suspected that the administration had tried to undermine the program.

The fundamental problems of Superfund, however, stem from decisions made in Congress before the Reagan administration arrived and from implementation by intelligent, highly motivated individuals, most of them acting in good faith. The troublesome results reflect several incentive and information problems built into our governmental system, exaggerated by the absence of the discipline normally provided by the budget process and the checks and balances that control other government programs.

"Polluter Pays" Is Violated

Superfund was sold to Congress on the principle of "polluter pays." Cleanup of dangerous waste sites would be paid for by those responsible for the problem. But this principle is routinely violated. The three taxes that pay for the administration of the program (a chemical tax, a petroleum tax, and an environmental income tax on large firms) violate the concept. Companies that may have never contaminated any waste site requiring cleanup must pay the tax. A firm that found a way to produce the same products with no pollution whatever would still pay the same amount of tax. Production, not pollution, is taxed. Furthermore, the paperwork costs are very high.[10] The EPA treats accused polluters, or "potentially responsible parties," as wrongdoers. These are the parties, usually firms, that must pay cleanup costs if they can be found. Yet the EPA has no responsibility to prove that they were guilty of wrongdoing, that they polluted the site in question, or even that serious risks from pollution exist.

To determine whether a site must be cleaned up, EPA uses seriously biased estimates of risks. The EPA does not have to provide proof that the contamination in a Superfund site is posing harm—or even serious risk of harm—to anyone nearby. It can order cleanups and force payment for them without showing (or even claiming) that the health benefits from the cleanups will outweigh the costs or that the benefits will be attained at the lowest possible cost. Accused parties can do little to challenge the EPA's decisions, except at the very end of the remediation process (typically expected to be twelve years). Even then, the burden is on them to prove that the EPA has acted arbitrarily or capriciously or has violated its own procedures as listed in its National Contingency Plan. Sometimes so little risk is present to begin with that the cleanup itself may introduce more risk than it removes.

There is, in other words, little restraint on what the manager of a Superfund site can order and then require "potentially responsible parties" to pay for. Even if the payments demanded are unreasonable, or they pay for unnecessary actions, the EPA has stated clearly that the companies must pay them. In a *Federal Register* statement, the EPA said that defendants ordered to pay Superfund costs "cannot avoid payment of United States' costs on the grounds that such costs are 'unnecessary' or 'unreasonable.'"[11] And there is no dollar limit on the cost of cleaning up any site.

As long as the EPA follows the procedures it has written for itself, forcing those to pay who cannot prove that the EPA acted in an arbitrary or capricious manner, the Superfund site manager's decisions will have the force of law. Those forced to pay have no recourse to substantive review. Former Assistant Attorney General Roger Marzulla put it well when he said, "With only slight exaggeration, one government lawyer has described a . . . [CERCLA] trial as requiring only that the Justice Department lawyer stand up and recite: 'May it please the Court, I represent the government and therefore I win'" (quoted in Evans 1996, 2110).

In sum, the EPA can order a cleanup without having to show that

- Any harm or the serious threat of significant harm has been committed

- Any law was broken by those whom it forces to pay for cleanups

- The chemical contamination was actually caused by the "responsible parties"

- The cleanup was necessary or that it was done to a reasonable level or in a reasonable manner

Congress thus replaced common-law concepts with nearly unchecked bureaucratic control. Congress allowed the EPA to judge liability and prescribe remedies without requiring evidence and to recover its costs from those accused of pollution. And it drastically restricted the opportunity for those required to pay to have an independent legal review. As long as the EPA follows the procedures it wrote for itself, its orders are the law. Furthermore, it financed a large portion of the program through special industrial taxes, rather than the normal budget process.

During the months preceding the passage of the original Superfund law, a few lone voices were heard questioning this abrogation of normal rights. Senator Alan Simpson, for example, said:

> It does alarm me to see the tendency, with but a sweep of the drafter's pen, to simply brush off on the floor many of the rules of evidence which have been so closely crafted and observed in our procedural life as lawyers. . . . The rules are there for a purpose. They have "come through the fires" and have been tempered by litigation. They do work. Basic reason and common sense should be the impetus behind their revision—not simply frustration.[12]

But such voices were overcome by the stampede.

No Due Process for "Polluters"

A key duty of any national government is to protect its citizens from wrongful harms imposed by others. But the power to protect must be restrained, or else the protectors may themselves impose serious harms.

To convict an accused criminal, the government (the police and the prosecutor) must overcome a heavy burden of proof—guilt beyond a reasonable doubt—following strict rules of evidence. Civil suits under common law (the kind that traditionally would have been brought by Love Canal residents) require a lighter burden, but the case must still be proven. The plaintiff must show, by the preponderance of evidence, that the defendant has caused harm or undue risk of harm. The court will not order a remedy until it is convinced that the complaint against the defendant is more likely to be right than wrong.

As we have seen, *no* burden of proof and *no* rules of evidence exist to protect those accused as responsible parties in the Superfund process. To see why this is wrong, consider the following. Suppose that a police department were allowed to decide who is guilty of sexual offenses or who might harbor tendencies that the police think pose a risk to others. Suppose that the police could require such individuals to take "remedial actions" (attending educational classes and costly, time-consuming counseling sessions, for example), all at their own expense. And suppose that the police were not required to obtain approval from a judge or jury and that the defendant could not demand a legal review of the police orders until all "remedial actions" were complete. Financial relief might be possible, but even that would be granted only upon proof that the police had acted in an arbitrary or capricious fashion. As long as they followed a system providing some "plausible connection" between the actions they ordered and some degree of increased public safety, the police would be vindicated.

Such a policy for dealing with an accused criminal, however serious the crime might be, would not be acceptable in the United States. Yet the above is a summary of how the EPA, under Superfund, treats those accused of contaminating sites. With Superfund, protections for those connected with a contaminated site were swept away. We should not be surprised that the Superfund program, operating much like the police in the above experiment, leads to excesses.

Risk Assessments—on the Wild Side

These violations of traditional legal rights would have a much narrower impact if it were not for the process that the EPA uses to determine the level of cleanup for a Superfund site. The EPA's risk assessment process uses assumptions and procedures that enormously magnify a site's possible risk. By exaggerating the specified risk, the EPA ropes in sites where no balanced review of the evidence would justify costly remediation.

Residents can be terrified or outraged, and accused parties can be pressed into paying bills for expensive cleanups based on only speculative claims of risk. On average, each cleanup costs $30 million. A more balanced and less biased risk assessment process of the sort that common law might require would lead to fewer fears by residents and fewer costly cleanups.

To launch these multimillion-dollar cleanups, the EPA does not have to prove that any harm exists. Instead, the EPA determines whether a *risk* of harm, either now or in the future, might be plausibly expected to exist for people living near the site or on it. The EPA procedures for estimating this risk are deliberately designed to be "conservative," meaning that they are heavily weighted toward extra caution. They are deliberately designed to overstate the true risk—to be extrasafe.

These extra margins of safety are piled one on top of another, causing serious distortion in the perception of risk by those who see the final risk estimates (see Belzer 1991). Consider how the EPA exaggerated the specified risks at one site, Idaho Pole, in Bozeman, Montana.

Sometime before 1978 pentachlorophenol (or PCP), a chemical preservative used to treat wooden utility poles, was spilled at the Idaho Pole Company facility in Bozeman, Montana. To clean it up, EPA officials insisted on a plan that would cost $9 million, a lot of money for a thirty-three-acre site in a small Montana city.

People were understandably frightened. An EPA study of the Idaho Pole site said that

> PCP is readily absorbed when it comes in contact with a person's digestive or respiratory system or the skin. Exposure to large amounts of PCP in a short time may result in profuse sweating, fever, weight loss, gastrointestinal irritation, lung, eye, and liver and kidney damage. Longer-term effects include a higher incidence of low-grade infections and depressed kidney function. PCP has been recently identified as a probable human carcinogen.

This statement was quoted in numerous front-page articles in the local newspaper (Haines 1991, 1; 1992a, 1; 1992b, 1). Clearly, the implication is that the chemical is quite dangerous to people nearby.

But the laboratory tests used to assess PCP's carcinogenic effects exposed mice (not people) to between fifty and four hundred times the amount of PCP that people might be exposed to at the Idaho Pole site, even using the EPA's extreme exposure assumptions. To determine the possible exposure of future residents, the EPA assumed that the site would be used as a mobile home park. There is no reason to believe this would happen, especially since the local government would have to change the zoning. The EPA also assumed that these hypothetical mobile home residents will not use the city water supply, even though it serves the site and is currently the source of water. Instead, the EPA said, the residents will drill private wells into contaminated water at the site and drink only that water in their homes. Also, according to the EPA, these residents will consume two hundred grams of contaminants every day throughout the year by eating homegrown produce, despite Montana's brief ninety-day growing season.

The EPA made other conservative and questionable assumptions: To figure out how contaminated with PCP the area was, the EPA measured its concentration in the groundwater at a house where no one lives that is owned by the Idaho Pole Company. Yet the contamination at that site formed the basis for figuring out the levels that future residents might be exposed to. Fully half of the PCP exposure that the hypothetical residents would experience by water came from shower fumes. Yet PCP does not vaporize (and thus cannot be inhaled) at the boiling point of water, much less at the temperature of shower water. The EPA ignored the fact that, even without human intervention, PCP is destroyed over time by microorganisms naturally present in soil and water. A publication of the EPA's own Office of Toxic Substances says that half of any PCP contamination present in water will be removed naturally every twenty to two hundred days.[13] In other words, the PCP is being destroyed naturally at a rather rapid rate.

Finally, the EPA claimed that a child living near the site faced more than a fifty-fifty chance (5.6 out of 10.0) of contracting cancer as a result of the site. But this claim was obsolete as soon as it was made. It was based on the existence of dioxin at the site, but the levels of dioxin were so low that the EPA officially eliminated them from consideration (they may have been a testing error). Yet the site report presented to Bozeman citizens continued to report this alarming risk estimate.

Tunnel Vision—Why an Agency Goes to Extremes

You might think that responsible public servants would recognize that this exaggeration and the policies it encourages are costly, wasteful, and counterproductive. But, for the most part, they do not. "Tunnel vision" comes into play.

Each government agency or bureau, including the EPA, is dedicated to a narrow mission. The EPA's mission is to protect against possible harm from pollution. It is not likely to weigh this mission against other agencies' goals. EPA officials are not likely to worry about whether spending more money reducing environmental risks means spending less on protecting endangered species. As Supreme Court justice Stephen Breyer (1993, 10) has put it, each agency will have "tunnel vision."

Agency officials will try to push beyond the point at which the broader public would—if the public were fully informed—want them to stop. In Breyer's words, tunnel vision is a "classic administrative disease" that arises "when an agency so organizes or subdivides its tasks that each employee's individual conscientious performance effectively carries single-minded pursuit of a single goal too far, to the point where it brings about more harm than good" (Breyer 1993, 11). In the environmental field, this pursuit, when unchecked, leads to standards that are so strict that meeting them demands enormous amounts of time, effort, and money that would be better spent somewhere else. Breyer calls this trying to achieve "the last 10 percent" (Breyer 1993, 11).

EPA pursues the last 10 percent more than most agencies. The uncertainties associated with environmental damages—the same uncertainties that make common-law approaches to environmental problems difficult—allow enormous speculation about the potential benefits of reducing pollution. With other regulations, such as those designed to reduce traffic deaths or deaths from acute poisoning, the approximate number of potential victims is fairly easy to estimate. By contrast, knowledge about harms such as cancer from environmental pollution is extremely uncertain. The best scientific estimates to date indicate that only about 2 percent of all cancers in the United States are caused by pollutants (see Doll and Peto 1981; Gough 1990). The EPA, however, can produce large risk estimates by speculating about potential victims.

The Superfund program is especially prone to tunnel vision. The focus of the Superfund program is far narrower even than the mission of the EPA. The job of Superfund is to protect citizens and their property against harm from hazardous wastes. Superfund managers are likely to ignore the costs forced on those outside the program, on the rest of the EPA, and, in some cases, on those they are trying to help.

Sites in Triumph, Idaho, and Aspen, Colorado, illustrate the effects of tunnel vision. Extensive mine tailings underlie much of these two towns. The EPA's conservative methodology predicted high levels of lead in the blood of the townspeople. After many years of living there, however, the residents' blood tests show no such result. In fact, lead levels are lower than the national average.[14] Nevertheless, in the face of strong local opposition, the EPA wants to clean up the sites, disrupting life in the towns for years to come. The EPA contends that possibly in the future someone could be harmed by the lead and arsenic in these tailings, ignoring the fact that the minerals are tied up in the mine tailings so that they are not very accessible to the residents, except when the tailings are disturbed, ground up, or broken. (Using heavy equipment to remove the tailings would inevitably disturb the tailings, putting some of the ground-up dust into the air.) Yet EPA officials have been adamant about the need for remediation.

As we have seen, Superfund risks are typically estimated by assuming that people live on the site or will move to the site and face "reasonable maximum exposure." Imagined future exposures are an important part of the rationale for Superfund cleanup. A study of a sample of seventy-seven Superfund sites revealed that more than 91 percent of the estimated cancer risk would accrue only to people who might move near the site in the future, not to actual individuals at the site (see Viscusi and Hamilton 1994). Simply restricting the future use of contaminated land could avoid these exposures. By taking a conservative approach and by imagining future activities that would maximize the exposure to pollutants, a Superfund site risk assessment can make a mountain out of a pollution molehill.

Indeed, Superfund site managers have shown themselves willing to ignore orders from EPA headquarters. Alan Carpien, an EPA Superfund attorney for nearly the full life of the program, said in a letter to the *Washington Times* that even directives from the White House could not force Superfund managers to change their risk assessment procedures to include cost-benefit analysis.

> From personal experience I know that my colleagues will continue to ignore risk-assessment guidelines, and high-level managers will not require subordinates to comply. Unless the law imposes legal obligations, EPA's behavior will not change.[15]

A site manager may simply be trying to justify as many resources for cleanup as possible to best protect the local people and their resources. The costs to the nation, to EPA as an agency, and to the Superfund program as a whole become secondary to the protection at the site itself.

The High Cost of Tunnel Vision

Tunnel vision helps explain why the EPA produces its benefits—primarily health and safety—at a high cost. Just how high these costs are was shown by a recent study conducted by Tammy Tengs of Duke University and others. They examined 587 regulations and other programs designed to save lives, measuring the regulations in terms of the cost per life year extended. (That is, if a regulation prevents the premature death of a person who would have died ten years later of other causes, then it has preserved ten life years. A regulation that prevents the premature death of an infant expected to live a full seventy years has preserved seventy life years.)

On average, the cost of each life year extended for a Federal Aviation Administration regulation was $23,000. For Occupational Safety and Health Administration regulations designed to reduce fatal accidents, the average was $88,000. But for the EPA, each environmental regulation cost $7,600,000 for each additional life year extended (see Tengs et al. 1995). Superfund program regulations were not evaluated in this study (one reason is that the EPA does not even systematically estimate the risk reductions from Superfund). But if such estimates were made, we might expect even higher cost figures.

Solving the Superfund Problem

The Superfund "shortcut" has proven to be a disastrous departure from the legal principles and traditions developed over the past several centuries. This trampling of legal traditions and rights has caused the extensive and costly problems that virtually all observers have noted.

Solving these problems is not a matter of tinkering with Superfund rules or even just clarification by Congress of the goals of the program, although clarification will certainly be needed. Only with the restoration of checks and balances can the program's excesses be brought under control.

The following principles should guide reform:

- Polluters must stop ongoing pollution when the rights of others are being violated, that is, when a person is involuntarily subjected to levels of harm or risk that exceed those commonly tolerated from other activities imposing involuntary risks (such as operation of motor vehicles, communicable diseases, etc.).

- Polluters must pay for damages they have caused and for cleanups necessary to avoid ongoing violations of the rights of others.

- Those who do not violate rights should not be singled out to pay for cleanups.

- Any agency that forces others to pay for cleanups must first prove responsibility for the pollution to be remedied and prove that the ordered actions are justified. Those who demand their right to a judicial review should not be forced to prove that EPA has been arbitrary and capricious; nor should they be forced to pay punitive "treble damages" merely because they sought legal review and did not prevail.

- In true emergency situations, public-works emergency removals may be justified but should be selected and administered by local and state governmental units.

- The right to an impartial judicial review should be available both to those accused of imposing harm or risk and to those claiming to be victims of pollution or of risk.

- Local governments should be recognized as having primary responsibility for control of local hazardous waste problems.

To restore these principles, I recommend two kinds of changes. One is to return to a legal regime that protects victims and potential victims of pollution while also protecting innocent parties accused of causing harm. That means abolishing Superfund. A less ambitious step to correct the excesses of Superfund is limiting the EPA's discretionary control, forcing it to adhere more closely to common-law principles.

Back to the Common Law

The common-law approach should not have been abandoned in 1980 when Superfund was enacted. The risks and harms from hazardous waste disposal sites are local, and, typically, only a few defendants are likely to cause harm or pose excessive risk. These factors make reliance on common-law courts appropriate at most hazardous waste sites.

People can obtain redress in the courts under common law for harm from pollution. For example, courts have held companies and individuals liable for damage from oil leaking from underground storage tanks (Hayward 1994, 631). A return to the common law would work as well as any principled approach can, given the uncertainty about the harms inflicted by hazardous waste.

When harm is alleged from a hazardous waste site, both possible victims and accused polluters should have their day in court. The rights of both should be protected, and the side favored by the preponderance of the evidence should win. Such a regime might result in fewer cleanups, but the sites not cleaned would be those where evidence of potential harm is lacking.

An advantage of common law is that, when protecting these rights imposes a costly cleanup duty on a polluter, there may be a way to make both parties better off. Suppose that the contamination threatens a water well and that remediation would cost $2 million. The polluter has no right to pollute the water. But the well's owner could sell his or her water rights. Perhaps, instead of paying the $2 million, the polluter offers to buy the right to unpolluted water for $1 million. This might be attractive to the owner. If it is not, the offer must be raised or the cleanup must be done. The point is that, when rights are clear, voluntary trades can reduce the cost to society of dealing with pollution.

Yes, common law is imperfect. Yet the shortcut that Superfund took around the problems with common law has caused more problems than it cured. Consider how each of the five complaints against the common law have fared under Superfund:

- *Lack of proof.* Superfund removed the requirement for proof of harm or undue risk based on rules of evidence and with the assurance of judicial review. This led to excesses by zealous bureaucrats pursuing their goals with tunnel vision.

- *Lack of consistency.* Site managers under Superfund are only loosely controlled by EPA headquarters, which itself is subject to constant political pressure. No one claims that the thousands of potential cleanup sites are treated consistently.

- *Lack of public protection.* Common law was indeed intended to protect private parties by dealing with specific pollution problems. But just as market transactions between individuals serve the whole community, common-law remedies set precedents that protect the entire community.

- *High costs.* Superfund litigation is time-consuming and immensely expensive, drawing in parties who have only a peripheral connection with alleged harms and risks.

- *Complexity of issues.* Under Superfund, the uncertainty remains but is largely ignored. Speculation and suspicion are sufficient to justify the expenditure of tens of millions of dollars per site.

Common-law remedies could be supplemented by an "emergency removals" program similar to the short-term program that Superfund operates today for genuine emergencies. It should be run by the state government, not the federal government, because the harms and the benefits of any site will nearly always be local, not national, in scope. If those in the jurisdiction receiving the benefits choose not to remediate, there is little reason why federal taxpayers should be asked to do so.

True emergencies at sites posing a large and immediate danger could be handled quickly. If the emergency removals did not correct the problem, more extensive cleanup could be ordered by a court or conducted as a local or state public works project, as funds are available.

Such remediation could be carried out mote efficiently by the private sector. I have previously recommended that Superfund sites for which no solvent responsible party exists be privatized (Stroup 1989; see also DeLong 1995 and Inhaber 1990). Some sites are potentially valuable enough to be sold to the highest bidder for cleanup or containment. In other cases, when the cost of necessary remediation exceeds the value of the property, the state or municipality could offer to pay a private owner to take over responsibility. Companies or individuals could bid; the lowest bidder would get the land.

The new owner would be liable for any damage caused to neighbors. The state or local government could also require the potential owner to post a bond to ensure that neither governments nor local residents are stuck with the cost of continued maintenance. The bond would be returned to the owner once the site was clean or permanently secure from leakage and off-site damage (the interest would accrue to the owner in the meantime).

Restraints on the EPA

Although returning to common-law principles is the ideal, several smaller steps could change the Superfund program to reflect more of our common-law heritage and thus impose the checks and balances needed to bring justice and rationality to the program. None of the prominently discussed proposals for amending Superfund does this. Specifically, Congress should

- Return to the liability provisions that are normally reflected in common law. In some cases, these may include strict liability and joint and several liability. The burden of proof should be on those demanding remediation to show that the accused caused unacceptable harm or risk of harm. Companies or individuals should not be required to pay for cleanups unless their actions violated the rights of others.

- Eliminate the three special taxes that support Superfund. They are not based on current or past pollution, and compliance is extremely costly relative to the revenues received. The EPA should compete with other government agencies through the normal congressional appropriations process to obtain money for dealing with hazardous wastes.

- Risk assessment procedures, when used to justify actions billed to others, should be reviewable in court. The EPA should report unbiased risk estimates, not just upper-bound estimates.

- At hazardous waste sites, the threshold for intolerable risks (that is, risks that must be reduced) should be similar to the threshold for other involuntary risks under regulation. Risks imposed on the public from carriers of contagious disease or from driving while impaired by known medical problems, for example, are comparable. Under current regulations, people on the ground face a risk of death from falling airplanes. That risk is low and tolerated. Yet the EPA often sets standards of risk at Superfund sites that are tighter than this. It tries to make sure that a person near a Superfund site faces a risk of death from cancer that is lower than the risk of a person on the ground dying from a falling airplane.

- There should be judicial review before remediation is imposed, and the EPA should be required to show by the preponderance of evidence that an unacceptable risk exists before starting remediation. Emergency removal should be subject to the more streamlined review typical of other emergency situations.

Conclusion

In sum, radical change in Superfund is vital. The Superfund shortcut is slow, often ineffective, inefficient, and unjust. It is also breeding hatred and contempt for the very public policies and public servants whose goals are to protect citizens from harm. The actions of overreaching bureaucrats, however well-intended, are earning the scorn and the ire of many.

To restore respect for the public servants who are supposed to be protecting citizens, I recommend a return to common law to solve problems stemming from chemicals and other substances at hazardous waste sites. Common law begins with justice, in the form of recognizing rights and requiring their protection. Efficiency comes second, as rights to locations and resources are traded in order to avoid both rights violations and unnecessary costs. When the pattern of rights is known from previous decisions, potential polluters are on notice and seek to avoid both liability and high-cost, after-the-fact fixes. They seek safer processes, better precautions, and safer locations for any risk that remains.

If such a restoration of rights is not feasible, then we must seek a close substitute: changes in the current Superfund program that will restore the rights normally guaranteed under our legal system. That means restoring judicial review, financing Superfund with congressional appropriations rather than special taxes not based on pollution, and revising the EPA's risk assessment procedures (while allowing affected parties the right to judicial review of those procedures).

Such changes are essential if the Superfund program is to be effective, fair, and perceived as fair. Not only are the health and the wealth of the nation at stake, but the very legitimacy of our government is on the line.

Notes

1. Reported in the *Los Angeles Times*, May 10, 1993.

2. See EPA, "National Priorities List for Uncontrolled Hazardous Waste Sites," 61 *Federal Register* 30510 (1996).

3. See EPA, "National Priorities List for Uncontrolled Hazardous Waste Sites," 60 *Federal Register* 20330 (1995).

4. See EPA, "Recovery of Costs for CERCLA Response Actions," 57 *Federal Register* 34,755 (1992). The indirect-cost figure of $412 was derived by taking the

$328.80, the simple average of costs across the ten regions, and updating to 1994 dollars using the CPI-U, all items.

5. These five points are presented in Harris, Want, and Ward (1987, 52 and 55).

6. Kemp's statement was made at the Joint Hearings before the Subcommittees on Environmental Pollution and Resource Protection of the Committee on Environment and Public Works, U.S. Senate (96th Congress), March 28–29, 1979, a field hearing at Niagara Falls, New York.

7. See *Voluntary Purchasing Groups, Inc. (VPG) v. Reilly (USEPA)* (U.S. Court of Appeals, 5th Circuit, 1989).

8. The full title is "Comprehensive Environmental Response, Compensation, and Liability Act of 1980."

9. A PRP ("potentially responsible party") can challenge in court an EPA decision to list a site on the National Priorities List. But at that point the EPA claims only that the site should be considered for possible cleanup. To get relief, the PRP must show that the EPA's decision to list the site is arbitrary and capricious, so such challenges seldom succeed. A PRP can also refuse an EPA order to clean a site, but it must show that the decisions it challenges were arbitrary or capricious; otherwise it must pay for the cleanup plus treble damages.

10. One tax, for example, brought in $520 million in 1990, but it "may impose on firms compliance costs that are more than four times the revenue collected," according to Katherine N. Probst et al. (1995, 62).

11. See EPA, "Recovery of Costs for CERCLA Response Actions" 57 *Federal Register* 34,755 (1992).

12. The statement is from "A Legislative History of the Comprehensive Environmental Response, Compensation, and Liability Act of 1980 (Superfund), Public Law 96-510," 97th Cong., 2d Sess., ser. no. 97-14, v. 1, 117.

13. These figures are from "SARA 313 Ecological Fact Sheet," U.S. Environmental Protection Agency, Office of Toxic Substances, mimeo.

14. Data are from a memo to "EPA, ATSDR, and Other Interested Parties" from Steve West of the Office of Environmental Health in the State of Idaho's Department of Health and Welfare, Division of Health, August 5, 1993, and "Testimony of Thomas S. Dunlop, Director of the Aspen/Pitkin Environmental Health Department, Aspen, Colorado concerning Smuggler Mountain Superfund Site Health Risk Assessment" to Committee on Public Works and Transportation, Subcommittee on Investigation and Oversight, U.S. House of Representatives, Washington, D.C., June 9, 1992.

15. Alan Carpien, letter to the editor of the *Washington Times,* June 18, 1995; Carpien made clear that he did not speak for the EPA.

References

Belzer, Richard B. 1991. "The Peril and Promise of Risk Assessment." *Regulation* 14(4): 40–49.

Breyer, Stephen. 1993. *Breaking the Vicious Circle.* Cambridge, Mass.: Harvard University Press.

Danzo, Andrew. 1988. "The Big Sleazy: Love Canal Ten Years Later." *Washington Monthly*, September, pp. 11–17.

DeLong, James. 1995. "Privatizing Superfund: How to Clean Up Hazardous Waste." *Policy Analysis* 247 (December 18).

Dixon, Lloyd S., Deborah S. Drezner, and James K. Hammit. 1993. *Private-Sector Cleanup Expenditures and Transaction Costs at 18 Superfund Sites.* Santa Monica, Calif.: Rand Institute of Civil Justice.

Doll, Sir Richard, and Richard Peto. 1981. *The Causes of Cancer.* New York: Oxford University Press.

Evans, William D., Jr. 1996. "The Phantom PRP in CERCLA Litigation: EPA to Rescue?" *Environment Reporter* 26(43): 2110.

Gough, Michael. 1990. "How Much Cancer Can EPA Regulate Away?" *Risk Analysis* 10(1): 1–6.

Haines, Joan. 1991. "Health Hell?" *Bozeman Daily Chronicle*, March 20, p. 1.

———. 1992a. "Health at Risk?" *Bozeman Daily Chronicle*, March 23, p. 1.

———. 1992b. "Did It Cause Cancer?" *Bozeman Daily Chronicle*, April 12, p. 1.

Harris, Christopher, William L. Want, and Morris A. Ward. 1987. *Hazardous Waste: Confronting the Challenge.* New York: Forum Books.

Hayward, Allison Rittenhouse. 1994. "Common Law Remedies and the UST Regulations." *Boston College Environmental Affairs Law Review* 21(4): 619–65.

Inhaber, Herbert. 1990. "Hands Up for Toxic Waste." *Nature* 347(6294): 611–12.

Landy, Marc K., Marc J. Roberts, and Stephen R. Thomas. 1990. *The Environmental Protection Agency: Asking the Wrong Questions.* New York: Oxford University Press.

Prestley, Peter B. 1995. "Superfund in Limbo." *ABA Journal*, June, p. 58.

Probst, Katherine N., Don Fullerton, Robert E. Litan, and Paul R. Portney. 1995. *Footing the Bill for Superfund Cleanups.* Washington, D.C.: Brookings Institution and Resources for the Future.

Stroup, Richard L. 1989. "Hazardous Waste Policy: A Property Rights Perspective." *Environment Reporter* 20(21): 868–73.

Tengs, Tammy O., Miriam Adams, Joseph Pliskin, Dana Fafran, Joanna Siegel,

Milton Weinstein, and John Graham. 1995. "Five Hundred Life-Saving Interventions and Their Cost-Effectiveness." *Risk Analysis* 15(3): 369–90.

Viscusi, Kip, and James Hamilton. 1994. "Superfund and Real Risks." *American Enterprise* 5(2): 36–45.

Wildavsky, Aaron. 1995. *But Is It True? A Citizen's Guide to Environmental Health and Safety Issues*. Cambridge, Mass.: Harvard University Press.

Zuesse, Eric. 1981. "Love Canal: The Truth Seeps Out." *Reason* 12(10): 16–33.

Appendix—Superfund: What Others Say

"This has been the most frustrating and most difficult experience of our lives. The Environmental Protection Agency (EPA) has changed us from card-carrying members of the environmental community into people who have no faith in the environmental protection currently being administered in our country. We believe that Superfund and the Environmental Protection Agency and CERCLA-Superfund have jointly become the environmental tragedy of all of the people. The EPA is spending billions of dollars of our money, to make lawyers rich, and the environment is paying the price. Nothing is getting cleaned up, and communities like ours are ruined for nothing."

> —Public comment by Donna Rose, Ken Raabe,
> and other concerned citizens of Triumph,
> Idaho, August 9, 1993.

"Under . . . Superfund legislation, pinning the bill on companies has acquired higher priority than ensuring the protection of public health."

> —"Cleaning Up Old Pollution," *The Economist*,
> February 29, 1992, p. 18.

"In some cases, unnecessary or inappropriate remediation might create more of a hazard than would be caused by leaving such materials undisturbed."

> —National Research Council, *Environmental
> Epidemiology, Public Health and Hazardous
> Wastes* (Washington, D.C.: National Academy
> of Sciences, 1991), p. 20.

"Of the estimated $4.2 billion spent each year on hazardous waste sites in the U.S., less than 1 percent has been devoted to the evaluation of health risks at these sites."

—National Research Council, 1991, p. 61.

"I have found no one—not a single person—at EPA, in the business community or in environmental groups, in universities or elsewhere, who has answered the following question affirmatively: If given $8.5 billion to spend on protection of health and the environment, should it all be devoted to the cleanup of hazardous waste disposal sites?"

—Paul R. Portney, "Reforming Environmental Regulation: Three Modest Proposals," *Issues in Science and Technology*, winter 1988, p. 79.

"Since its inception at the end of 1980, Superfund has received a great deal of money, over $5 billion so far, to clean up the nation's worst toxic waste sites. But OTA's research, analysis, and case studies support the view shared by most observers—including people in affected communities and people in industry paying for cleanups—that Superfund remains largely ineffective and inefficient. Technical evidence confirms that, all too frequently, Superfund is not working environmentally the way the law directs it to. This finding challenges all those concerned about human health and the environment to discover what is wrong and fix it."

—Office of Technology Assessment, *Are We Cleaning Up? 10 Superfund Case Studies* (Washington, D.C.: U.S. Congress, June 1988), p. 1.

Environmental Regulation: Lessons from the Past and Future Prospects

On the frontispiece of Rachel Carson's powerful book *Silent Spring* (1962), one finds a quotation from Albert Schweitzer: "Man has lost the capacity to forestall and foresee. He will end by destroying the earth." Schweitzer's words seemed entirely appropriate to Carson's significant work, one of the first modern efforts to call attention to uncontrolled activities that were damaging the environment. Although later scientists offered strong rebuttals to Carson's assault on DDT, the principal focus of her story, most would agree that *Silent Spring* helped usher in a new environmental era as Americans turned to regulation in the hope of avoiding, or at least postponing, Schweitzer's pessimistic forecast (Whelan 1985).

During the 1970s and 1980s, the United States built one of the largest regulatory enterprises the world has ever witnessed, much of it in the name of environmental protection. The thrust of the 1970s is shown by the increased number of pages in the U.S. *Federal Register*, a daily government publication that announces new and revised regulations (see fig-

This chapter is based on a forthcoming paper submitted to *Journal des Economistes et des Etudes Humaines* (1997).

Figure 1   Federal Register Pages: 1940–1994 (in thousands)

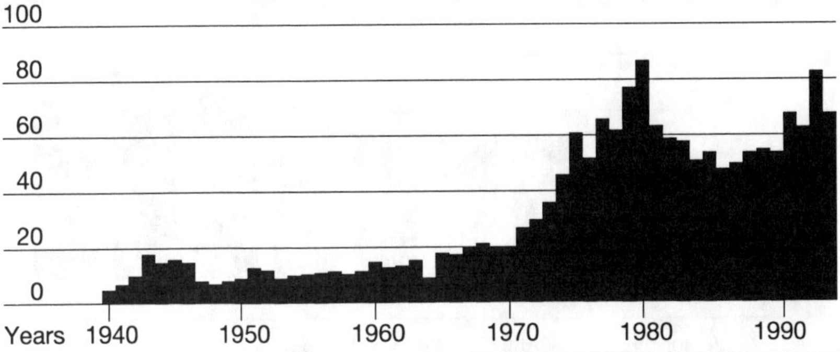

SOURCE: *Federal Register* for calendar years.

ure 1). From 1970 forward, a rising tide of regulation encompassed every feature of American life, focusing particularly on environmental safety and health. The size of the workforce at the U.S. Environmental Protection Agency, formed in 1970 to become America's environmental caretaker, also increased (see figure 2). Clearly, environmental protection was a growth industry until the 1980s, when the Reagan administration reversed the trend.

The move to national regulation marked an abrupt change in the way Americans had previously managed environmental quality. Before the 1970s, natural resources and the environment were protected first by private law—property rights enforced in common law courts, supplemented by state and local ordinances and multistate compacts. Indeed, at the time the EPA was being formed, in 1970, air pollution and other environmental statutes were in place in each of the fifty states (Portney 1990a, 29). After 1970, environmental resources were protected by public laws written by politicians and enforced across the nation.

If the move to federal regulation was about improving the environment, an examination of the record raises serious questions about the changes that followed (Portney 1990a, 40–51). Relative to 1970, environmental quality is improved or at least no worse. But huge amounts have been spent on command-and-control regulation. Estimates for 1990 indicate that the full costs of all federal regulation ranged between $434

Figure 2   EPA Workforce: Selected Fiscal Years
            (in thousands of workers)

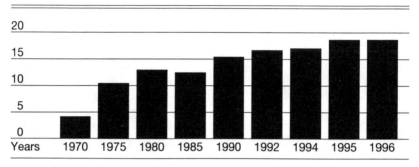

SOURCE: Center for the Study of American Business, St. Louis, Missouri

and $508 billion annually, or about $2,000 per U.S. citizen (see Hahn
and Hird 1991). Indeed, the 1990 regulatory costs imposed by the U.S.
Environmental Protection Agency alone are estimated to be $100 bil-
lion.[1] Beyond these amounts, the command-and-control regime fostered
by the national government has stifled innovation, blunted investment
in new plant capacity, and sharply reduced the ability of ordinary citizens
to manage their property. In a few words, individual freedom has been
sharply compromised.

   It is clear that representative democracies face severe challenges in
the search for effective, lower-cost ways to protect environmental quality;
the United States is still struggling to achieve that end. Given the extent
and magnitude of the U.S. experience, it seems obvious that a critical
analysis of that experience should offer some useful lessons to others
who may be just beginning to form national policies. To be most useful,
a review of the lessons must focus on problems encountered along the
way, difficult issues that have emerged, and patterns of behavior that
seem to typify the U.S. effort.

   This chapter, which reflects on the U.S. environmental saga, points
out failings, and offers suggestions for avoiding the costly policy decisions taken by Americans, begins with a discussion of the constitutional
fence that separates private and public decision making. Environmental
protection can rest on either side of the fence, which is to say control is
either a matter of law and market forces or a struggle with the rule of

politics. The section explains why the political alternative is attractive. The section that follows describes some of the more costly regulatory episodes, with attention paid to air, water, and hazardous waste pollution. We know that the ability to forestall and foresee is crucial to survival and prosperity. We also know that humans are learning animals. In the hope that something can be learned from all this, the last major section focuses on property rights alternatives and offers proposals for avoiding some of America's more costly policy actions.

The Constitutional Fence: Why Politics Prevails

FENCES AND PRIVATE PROPERTY

Robert Frost reminds us that there is something about a wall that makes it want to come down, and he was not just talking about gravity. He was referring to our free spirits and our desire to live an unconstrained life, to move freely and enjoy associations with humans and nature. But after making the point about walls, Frost concluded that "good fences make good neighbors." Why? Fences help us forestall. They force us to consider the consequences of our actions, to foresee. Fences curb our greed, the unfettered desire to gain without paying.

The U.S. Constitution established a stout fence that protects ordinary people from the unrestrained forces of government. It evolved from the personal constitutions of ordinary people, by and large farmers—the first conservationists—who had already gained liberty and had a deep distrust of central governments (Yandle 1992). Unlike most other nations of the world, the people who chose to form the union were sovereign when the nation was being formed. For a century or more they had lived under a rule of law—common law—brought with them from England.

Common law, which sets rules of conduct on the private side of the constitutional fence, was the law of the people, country people, not of government. Indeed, common law was referred to as the "law of the land," an appellation not given to statute law, which was the work of legislative bodies. The emergence of a rule of law had a long and tortuous history. In 1225, ordinary Englishmen were assured by the Magna

Carta that "no freeman shall be deprived of his free tenement or liberties or fee custom but by the law of the land." In 1635, the English Petition of Rights stated more simply, "Englishmen are free in their property, which cannot be taken by government." In more modern times, common-law rules protected landowners from pollution, noise, and any other damages that might be imposed by others. No government permit would allow one to impose harm on his neighbors. Common-law rules were simple and severe. If you polluted, you were ordered to pay damages or to shut down or both. The law of private nuisance protected private rights. It was joined by public nuisance law, which protected groups of people from pollution and other harm. Exclusive property rights protected individuals from encroachment by neighbor, stranger, ruler, and legislator.

The takings clause of the Fifth Amendment is a stark reminder that the Constitution would not have been ratified without assuring the sanctity of common-law rights. That clause brought forward the ancient law of the land: "Nor shall private property be taken for public use, without just compensation." But its spotty enforcement reminds us that there are no absolute absolutes. Private property rights define one side of the constitutional fence.[2] The public sector, public rights, and the rule of politics lie on the other side of the fence.

We should note that private property rights are not just legal conveniences that we might take or leave without penalty. Property rights emerged as part of a Darwinian survival process, not from a political or legal process. They did not arise with the Fifth Amendment in 1787, with the Petition of Right in 1635, or with the powerful language in the Magna Carta in 1225. Nor do they exist because the Supreme Court says so. Property rights were there all along; they evolved from the bedrock of communities of people who survived, and they are present even when not enforced. In short, the law of property is part of the evolutionary process. Private property, the right to exclude, is constantly being rediscovered.

The incentives that accompany private property rights play a crucial role in determining beneficial outcomes. First, in order to gain the goods and cooperation of another person, one must obtain permission. Doing that generally involves trade. That is, people give up things they control to obtain things others control. Gains from trade, markets, and specialization follow. Free market transactions are a product of exclusive property rights. When property rights are secure, the owner has an incentive to improve his assets, to maximize their value. The owner looks ahead, considers options, and seeks to assign his property to higher-valued uses. When successful, the owner reaps the reward. When unsuccessful, the owner bears the costs. Property rights cause people to conserve natural resources and guard scarce environmental assets. When another party imposes costs on or damages the owner's property, the owner can bring a common-law suit against the offending party. Private property rights enable the rights holder to foresee and forestall.

For decades, property rights and common law protected air and water quality in the United States. Thousands of suits were brought in cases that ranged from farmers suing paper mills, and winning, to states suing polluters in another state. The outcomes did not generate uniform environmental standards. In some locations, environmental quality was high and incomes were low. People in those regions more often than not accepted some pollution in order to gain income. Where environmental quality was low and incomes more plentiful, people were more inclined to sue when their environmental rights were abridged. Enforcement of environmental rights reflected the norms, traditions, and conditions of the community.

One last feature of property rights and common-law environmentalism needs to be emphasized. It is impossible for a special-interest group simultaneously to bring complaints to each and every common-law court in the country, hoping that judges will grant similar rulings. In short, an interest group, be it environmental or industrial, cannot obtain a national fix for a problem via common-law courts. Attempts to use the state's police power to restrict output or redistribute income will not work.

The Public Side of the Fence

Private rights, markets, voluntary exchanges, and opportunity costs dictate outcomes on one side of the constitutional fence. Politics, special interests, and redistribution describe activity on the other side. Under a representative government, citizens can organize and express their concerns to politicians. The politicians can write statutes that convert private to public property. In other words, social decisions can be moved from the private side of the fence to the political side.

The urge to move control of property to the public sector is practically irresistible. The rules of politics make it possible for interest groups to obtain benefits at no direct cost to themselves or at least to shift a significant portion of the cost to others. The successful interest group is typically tightly organized and small in number, relative to the body politic. Rules and regulations can transfer valuable benefits to each of the members of the small group while imposing small costs to each of the large number of citizens or consumers who ultimately bear the cost.

Incentives change when operating on the political side of the fence. Politicians logically seek to strengthen their positions, which means they will serve important interest groups. Unfortunately, what is good for a special-interest group seldom serves the broader interests of the general public. Private property rights and markets tend to place the cost of actions on those taking the actions. Benefits and costs are linked. Political redistribution breaks the linkage between costs and benefits. One group gets the benefits; another bears the costs. More often than not, the diverse bearers of the costs are rationally ignorant about the entire matter. The costs are disguised in prices and taxes.

Consider environmental protection, specifically air pollution control. The problem of harmful emissions that impose costs on unsuspecting parties is handled in a variety of ways worldwide. First, property rights can be defined and enforced at common law. Put simply, ordinary people have the right not to be harmed by uninvited emissions that fall on their bodies or their property. Under a rule of law and markets, this approach requires no standing body of bureaucrats, no regulations, and no political action, other than operating a strong court system. Obviously, the approach holds little appeal for polluters, politicians, and bureaucrats.

A second approach involves setting performance standards to be met by all polluters. In this case, politicians write statutes that set firm goals to be achieved by specific dates for specified pollutants, say an 85 percent reduction of sulfur dioxide emissions in ten years. A bureaucracy is involved in identifying the polluters, advising them of the rule, and monitoring compliance. The polluters must perform or suffer the consequences. This approach gives incentives for polluters to find the lowest-cost way of achieving the goal. Flexibility matters. But, as we shall see, the approach requires relatively little of bureaucrats and politicians. Rationally ignorant voters are not aware of the nice features of the approach, though they might like them if they knew about them.

A third approach involves placing taxes or fees on pollution and setting the rate of payment high enough to obtain the desired outcome. A bureaucracy for monitoring outcomes is again required, and, once again, the polluter has an incentive to minimize cost. Theoretically, there is little interaction between politicians and polluters. Once the fee or tax is set, market forces take over. This approach may be attractive to efficiency seekers, but it is not attractive to seekers of special favors and bureaucrats. There is yet another problem to consider. It is easy to say that taxes will be set at an appropriate level and that markets will take over from there. Taking other taxes as our cue, it is seldom that taxes are set with efficiency in mind and obvious that taxes are never set once and for all. The process is political, thus providing another opportunity for special-interest groups to gain at the expense of less-powerful groups.

The last approach, which dominates representative democracies and forms the basis for practically all environmental regulation in the United States, involves setting national standards and then specifying precisely how the standards must be met for each and every industry, indeed for each of many machines within a given plant. Demonstrably the most costly way to regulate polluters, the approach calls for a large, highly trained bureaucracy that will apply engineering in the development of detailed rules to be followed by one and all. The bureaucracy expands.

Polluters generally dislike this approach; they are hamstrung with detailed rules. But note the word *generally* in the preceding sentence. Some polluters *love* the approach. When designed to their liking, command-and-control regulation can be profitable, such as when environmental rules set higher standards for new sources than for older ones. Operators of older plants are comforted by a federally enforced output restriction. Within the favored group, other gains are obtained when politicians apply the technologies already used by part of an industry, raising competitors' costs and leaving the lucky proponents with their cost structure untouched.

Of course, politics is the order of the day in all this. The politicians hear from all the polluters and the environmentalists as well. Each group attempts to influence the hand that writes the detailed legislation, and many are willing to support politicians that do them favors. The political churning consumes valuable resources. All else equal, production of consumer goods and services gives way to the production of rules and regulations reducing the formation of wealth.

In the United States, the rules adopted apply rigorously to new sources of pollution, while the older ones are allowed to operate with lighter controls. The strict standards generate barriers to entry, help keep existing industries in place, and assist politicians in the more mature industrialized regions. All along, environmentalists sing the praises of the politicians. They are the "Baptists" (see Yandle 1989). The polluters who gain competitive advantage are the "bootleggers." In the United States, Baptists and bootleggers have historically lobbied for laws that prohibit the Sunday sale of alcoholic beverages. The Baptists support the rules for religious reasons; the bootleggers want to have the market to themselves on Sunday.

We see technology-based, command-and-control regulation all about us. Yet we know that the other approaches are almost always less costly and more effective. The highly detailed safety regulations developed and enforced by the U.S. Occupational Safety and Health Administration provide a prime example. A high frequency of injuries in certain industries can be addressed in the ways described for pollution. Common-law suits can bring discipline; performance standards can be set. Taxes or other penalties can be levied. Detailed engineering standards can be devised and enforced that require each and every firm in every industry to do things in specified ways. Again, this approach is empty of efficiency-enhancing incentives. But, again, command and control yields opportunities for rents to be gained, bureaucracies to grow, and politicians to tell important interest groups that they are working to make things safer for working people.

The controversy over ozone depletion and the release of chloro-fluorocarbons (CFCs) illustrates bootleggers and Baptists at work in the market for regulation (see Bast, Hill, and Rue 1994). Unlike the previous example, however, this time the bureaucrats are the bootleggers. The potential problem involving the ozone layer and CFCs first arose in 1974, when two academic researchers put forward a theory connecting CFCs and ozone. According to their theory, all CFCs, which are extraordinarily light, will ultimately migrate to the stratosphere where they interact with and deplete the ozone layer.

The ozone layer is important to human health because it filters and reduces the strength of ultraviolet rays that might damage the skin. The publicity that accompanied the researchers' report led the EPA in 1978 to ban the use of CFCs as propellants for aerosol products. Although warnings were given, their use in refrigeration units and producing high-technology electronic products was not affected. All along the world awaited empirical verification of the ozone depletion theory. Some evidence was provided by two British scientists working in Antarctica in 1985 when they discovered an "ozone hole" in the upper stratosphere over the South Pole.[3] The presence of the hole suggested that the ozone layer was being depleted at a troublesome rate and that CFCs were the culprit. All this led to an international agreement in 1987 to cap, if not ban, the production of CFCs worldwide. Meanwhile the EPA went forward with phaseout rules for CFCs.

Long after the EPA moved to end the production of CFCs in the United States, *Time* magazine explained how National Aeronautics and Space Administration (NASA) scientists suppressed a report that showed the Antarctica ozone hole was a statistical artifact (see Bailey 1993). The *Time* story indicates that the thickness of the ozone layer is cyclical. Recovery had occurred *before* the EPA made its final decision, but NASA scientists suppressed the data.

But why would the scientists engage in such chicanery? According to *Time* magazine, the NASA activity was perfectly timed to "bolster the agency's budget requests for its global climate change program, whose funding was slated to double in 1993" (quoted in Bailey 1993, 119–20). In other words, NASA scare tactics brought funds to the bureaucrats and assisted the EPA's mission, all in the name of protecting the public interest. What about consumers? In 1993, the owners of 115 million older cars were warned that they would have to pay up to $1,000 to have their cars retrofitted for a new refrigerant. Analysts estimate that the phaseout costs will range from $23 billion to $36 billion (see Bast, Hill, and Rue 1993, 63).

Examining the Record

THE HIGH COST OF POLITICIZED
COMMAND-AND-CONTROL REGULATION

By now, the record is clear. The use of command-and-control regulation for managing environmental quality has left a deep imprint on the U.S. economy. As mentioned earlier, estimates for 1990 indicate that the full annual cost of all federal regulation ranged between $434 and $508 billion, or about $2,000 per person.[4] About half the billions spent on regulation relate to the environment. The 1990 costs of regulations imposed by the U.S. EPA alone are estimated at $100 billion (see Nelson 1993). Of course, the United States is a large, highly industrialized country. Have these expenditures delivered a large increase in environmental quality?

Keith Schneider, a national correspondent for the *New York Times*, has followed the actions by the EPA as closely as any single national observer. Writing in *ECO* magazine, Schneider reports the comments of William E. Cooper, an ecologist at Michigan State University who had examined the efforts in his state to deal with hazardous wastes (Schneider 1993). Cooper states, "If ever there was a textbook case of good intentions producing bad results, what's happening in this state with toxic waste law is it." Going on, Cooper adds: "We have a situation where laws meant to lower risks to the environment and health are raising them. Laws meant to help people are hurting them. It's a microcosm of a much larger problem this country is facing with environmental protection" (Schneider 1993, 17).

Anecdotal evidence is easy to find. Schneider tells about abandoned western mines where immense piles of tailing contain lead, sulfur, arsenic, and cyanide. These contaminants can leach into groundwater, causing trace amounts of pollutants to make their way into drinking water. The tailings impose a risk. The open mines pose another risk. Schneider reports that at least "162 people have been killed and hundreds more injured since the late 1970s in falls associated with unprotected mine shafts" (Schneider 1993, 18). Congress has chosen to deal extensively with the tailings problem, where risks are trivial. During the

1993–94 fiscal year, the government budgeted $10 billion for cleaning up tailings from abandoned mines. Less than $500 million was spent to close abandoned mines and restore land affected by mining operations.

Even the EPA agrees with the implications of these stories. In a widely distributed 1987 self-study, the EPA examined its wide-ranging regulatory activities, the budget allocated by Congress to each of them, and then ranked the relative riskiness of thirty-one problem areas addressed by the agency (U.S. Environmental Protection Agency 1987). Each of the thirty-one areas was evaluated for four types of risk: cancer risk, noncancer health risks, ecological effects, and welfare effects. In the study, seventy-five EPA staff members sought to determine how well the agency's efforts to reduce risk matched the riskiness of various problem areas. The report concluded that "the rankings of risk . . . do not correspond closely with EPA's statutory authorities" and "do not correspond well with EPA's current program priorities" (U.S. Environmental Protection Agency 1987, xix).

The long list of high-risk/low-effort activities provided in the report included indoor radon, indoor air pollution, nonpoint-source pollution, and accidental releases of toxic materials. By contrast, the report listed Superfund, municipal nonhazardous waste site cleanup, and cradle-to-grave regulation of toxic chemicals as high-budget items that deal with low risks. The report concluded that the EPA is hamstrung by politics.

In a 1991 *Fortune* magazine interview, William Reilly, EPA administrator during the Bush administration, was confronted with findings showing that as many as twenty thousand annual lung cancer deaths were associated with radon gas in homes and, by comparison, at most five hundred cancer deaths associated with all the nation's hazardous waste sites (Main 1991). At the time, the federal government was spending $100 million annually on radon control and some $6.1 billion annually to clean up hazardous waste sites. Reilly responded that environmental spending "cries out for discipline and rationality, for someone to put things in a reasonable hierarchy" (Main 1991, 95).

Based on this anecdotal evidence, one would be hard-pressed to recommend the regulatory approaches of the United States to some other nation. But these are anecdotes. Is there more to the story? During the last twenty years a number of major empirical studies have been completed to compare the cost of command-and-control regulation with a simpler approach that allows polluters to find the least-cost way to achieve a regulatory objective. In short, performance standards are compared with technology-based, command-and-control regulation. A summary of this research indicates that the ratio of costs for command and control to the more flexible approach ranges from a high of 22.0 to 1.0 to a low of 1.07 (Portney 1990b, 72–73). In between are ratios like 4.18, 5.96, and 14.4 to 1.0. In the extreme case, the environmental goal now being accomplished for $22 per unit could be achieved for $1 per unit. Command and control was always found to be more costly.

THE MONOPOLY PROBLEM

Common sense tells us that far less environmental cleanup will be accomplished when the highest-cost approaches are mandated by government. But common sense is obviously not the motivating factor when environmental protection is placed in the hands of a bureaucracy that monopolizes regulation. Fearful of monopoly in most quarters, the American people are more than content to have environmental protection monopolized by the national government and one regulatory agency—the U.S. Environmental Protection Agency.

Simple economic logic tells us that a monopolist will tend to restrict output and raise price. The choice of high-cost, command-and-control regulation places a high "price" on environmental quality. But is there evidence that the monopolist restricts output? And relative to what?

In his 1990 assessment of the record for air pollution, Paul R. Portney gave a comparison of gains in air quality before the formation of the EPA in 1970 and the record of accomplishments since then:

> If air quality had been deteriorating prior to 1970 but then began to improve, some contribution on the part of the amendments passed that year might be suggested. While air quality data extending back into the 1960s are less reliable than today's, they do tell an interesting story. According to data from the EPA, average ambient total suspended particulate levels fell about 22 percent between 1960 and 1970. During the period 1966 to 1971 annual average ambient SO_2 concentrations fell by an even larger 50 percent. While we must be leery of trends based on such a small number of sites, these data are important because they suggest that air quality was improving as fast or faster before the Clean Air Act as it has since that time

... this conclusion should give us pause in reflecting on the likely effects of the Clean Air Act. (Portney 1990a, 50–51)

Evidence of restricted output is also found when the national government record for water quality improvements is examined. In his 1993 survey of studies, Robert Nelson reported on water quality conditions in 1972, the year of the first federal command-and-control statute (Nelson 1993). Citing Conservation Foundation data, Nelson tells us that 64 percent of the stream miles and 84 percent of the lakes and reservoirs were meeting the 1972 water quality goals when the statute was passed. In other words, huge amounts have been spent on water that was already clean. Later reviews of improvements were not all that optimistic. Of course, many rivers are cleaner today than in 1972, and water quality generally has not deteriorated; but we should expect no less when $20 billion or so is spent each year in meeting the requirements of the statute.

The disturbing record of federal efforts taken to improve air and water quality is nothing compared with the record on hazardous waste cleanup. Since 1980, when the first Superfund program was initiated, the U.S. EPA has investigated 38,000 potential sites to determine whether they should be cleaned.[5] More than 3,500 emergency actions have been taken to deal with high-risk sites. And 1,320 sites have entered the full Superfund program for complete cleanup. At the end of September 1993, just 52 sites had been cleaned. On average, twelve years is required to jump the bureaucratic hurdles, handle the litigation, and proceed with cleaning away hazardous wastes. Congressional Budget Office estimates of the cost of cleaning all current and future Superfund sites run from $106 billion to $460 billion (Probst et al. 1995, 18).

What appears to be a bad situation is made far worse when the risks are considered. For the most part, Superfund sites are low risk. Extraordinary assumptions are made to get a site on the Superfund list.[6] To generate above-normal risks so that a site can enter the EPA's list, children are assumed to eat dirt from the site once a day for thirty-five years. In other cases, hunters are assumed to consume venison for thirty years from deer that have eaten grass growing on a contaminated site. Even then, the sites may just barely pass EPA muster.

To cap all this, the federal statute requires that runoff from a mitigated Superfund site pass the drinking water standard, which means that discharge from a site will generally be cleaner than the waters in receiving streams and lakes. The monopoly regulator appears to have raised price and restricted output.

There is still more to consider. The location of incinerators, landfills, and other obnoxious disposal activities in lower-income neighborhoods has generated another round of controversy. Instead of buying land outright and paying for harmful side effects, state governments can draw on their authority to preempt community zoning ordinances and use eminent-domain powers to locate the facilities among those who lack political power.

Is There a Better Way?

An examination of history and the record of other countries leaves the clear impression that there is a better way to protect environmental rights. Notice the words *environmental rights*. If environmental quality is to be improved and protected, environmental rights of one form or another must be defined and enforced. For the United States, tinkering with regulation will not do the job. New institutions will have to be formed, institutions that avoid the heavy hand of government and provide commonsense incentives to individuals. There is just no environmental protection alternative. But what can we learn from the experience of other countries?

RIGHTS-BASED RIVER BASIN MANAGEMENT

For decades and longer, water quality in France and Germany has been managed and protected by quasi-public river basin associations. Instead of relying on centralized command and control, these countries apply decentralized management based partly on economic incentives. The European organizations require all dischargers to make payments on the basis of the quality of their discharge. Some discharge is not allowed at all. But rights to water quality are protected for every member of the river basin associations, including municipalities, industry, and residents. (In an embryonic state, a river basin association is now operating in the United States that supports property rights to water quality and facilitates trade among point- and nonpoint-source dischargers.) In these cases, technology-based, command-and-control regulation is replaced with property rights and prices. As might be expected, politics still matters. And in some instances, we encounter a monopolist. But overall, the outcomes are superior to command and control by central authorities.

Germany passed the 1976 Federal Water Act and Effluent Charge Law with the objective of improving or maintaining water quality on the Ruhr River.[7] During the process of passage of the law, there was a struggle between the states and the federal government for control over the regulatory process and the type of regulatory mechanism to be implemented—uniform standards versus effluent tax. The effluent charge was adopted with a regulatory standard accompanying it. The federal government set standards and the states implemented effluent charges. It was thought that the people in the individual river basins of the Ruhr would be more knowledgeable and better equipped to set the effluent charges than the federal government. Typically, a river basin association is formed to manage water quality. In the case of the Ruhr, the effluent charges were set high enough to create marketlike incentives to abate.

Effluent fees are paid to the association by industries and municipalities and cover a wide range of pollutants. Payments are based on expected volume of total flow and the concentration of pollutant within the flow. The charges vary by industry type and across municipalities (see Hahn 1989, 105). The effluent fees pay for administrative costs of water quality management and finance water quality improvement projects (Hahn 1989, 105).

Membership in an association is not, however, voluntary for any particular discharger. The monopoly status of the authority and the limited choice available to the discharger lead to constrained efficiency with a high probability of monopoly output restrictions. To exit the system, a firm must exit Germany because all rivers are now organized along the same lines. It is difficult to assess the overall effects of the German system. The effluent charges induce cost-effective pollution control. Monopoly control of the rivers, however, can lead to higher fees and too little environmental use.

The river basin management system in France is similar to the one in Germany and has been in existence since 1969. Important features of the law include (1) six river basin agencies act as regional branches of the national government, (2) the agencies have the authority to implement individual programs of water quality management, and (3) the law emphasizes the use of a price instrument (effluent fee) to achieve water quality goals (Kneese and Bower 1984, 270). The charges cover a wide range of pollutants, with the revenues going toward projects to improve water quality and also for administrative expenses. The charge system improves environmental quality through allocation of charge revenues used for pollution abatement activities (Hahn 1989, 104).

The effluent fees are imposed on municipalities as well as on industry. Relative to the other European water management systems, France's effluent fees were initially set at low levels, typically assessed across the water basin, and then increased (Hahn 1989, 104). The charges are based on the expected level of discharge, not on actual performance. In that sense, the French effluent charges are more like taxes than effluent fees.

As with the German associations, a river basin committee is set up for each basin. Included on the committees are all water users, local communities, and administrative personnel, all having equal representation. One key to France's success with this program is found in the practice of setting initial charges at low levels and then gradually raising them. At present, the French authorities regulate agricultural discharge (nonpoint source) and build drainage systems and treatment plants for runoff from fields. The authority does not facilitate transactions among point-source dischargers.

The French system yields a monopoly regulator with taxing authority based indirectly on discharge. Polluters cannot exit the association, other than by relocating to another country, and they are not given a choice of control instruments. When compared with the German case, there is an even greater probability of output restrictions and high fees generated by the authorities' monopoly status because the fees are not linked directly to abatement-control costs.

Like people, institutions evolve, carrying with them elements of social learning. There is adaptation and selection. What about environmental management? Can the lessons learned from Europe be transported to the United States?

Perhaps. North Carolina's Tar-Pamlico Association, a group of point-source dischargers organized in 1989, became the first transacting water pollution–control trading community in North America.[8] The association, which is fundamentally a broker, emerged as a public-sector firm to reduce transaction costs among members, which, with one exception, are publicly owned treatment works (POTWs). After a series of regulatory events that began in 1986, EPA command-and-control regulation was relaxed for the POTWs and industrial dischargers who decided to join the association. The EPA's rule revision represented a significant regime shift.

Today, the transacting organization facilitates trade among member pollution dischargers and nonmember farmers. The farmers reduce field runoff and collectively reduce the discharge of phosphorous and nitrogen to the Pamlico estuary, a body of water that connects to the Atlantic Ocean.[9] The transactions among these point- and nonpoint-source polluters represent a distinguishing feature of the association.

Tar-Pamlico was initiated after a series of fish kills led local residents, fishermen, and environmental groups to push for state action to regulate nutrient discharge. The North Carolina Environmental Management Commission classified the Tar-Pamlico River Basin as nutrient-sensitive waters and set limits on the total phosphorous and nitrate discharged into the basin.

The constraint for the association was for all members' nutrient discharge combined to be 425,000 kilograms a year by the end of 1994, about 200,000 kilograms less than the current level. The association, which has consistently been below its annual nutrient constraint, is allowed to bank excess abatement for use when plants expand. Membership in the association is voluntary.

The combined resources and centralized information generated by the association led to the hiring of a consulting firm that evaluated each member's facility. It was discovered that operational adjustments at some member's facilities could further reduce nutrient loads for the association. By making marginal adjustments, nutrient loads were reduced without the purchase of capital-intensive pollution-control equipment. Through the employment of the consulting firm, overall nutrient loading to the watershed was reduced by 28 percent even though the average monthly flow to the watershed increased by 18 percent.

The annual combined limitations were imposed solely upon the association; other nonparticipating point sources must meet their own permit requirements. Collectively, point sources accounted for only 15 percent of the total nutrient load in the watershed. Some 85 percent of the nutrient discharge came from agricultural and other nonpoint sources. As part of their agreement with the North Carolina state government, the association agreed to fund a $400,000 computer model that simulates the flow of nutrients and forecasts the impact of nutrient removal. The computer model would help establish a total limitation for all dischargers within the watershed and target problem nonpoint-source areas.

The regulatory system uses both an effluent fee and marketable permits. The association, acting as a single entity, has the choice of internally reducing nutrient discharge or paying an effluent charge. The funds generated from effluent charges are then used to reduce nutrient loads of nonpoint sources. Farmers in the region are paid to adopt management practices that reduce nutrient runoff. An implicit system of marketable permits is also at work within the association. Members of the association have varying marginal nutrient abatement costs, leading to substantial gains from trade when members transact with one another. Indeed, one purpose of the consulting firm hired by the association was to equate the marginal nutrient abatement costs across all members.

In contrast with the European systems, Tar-Pamlico is a voluntary association. Transactions are facilitated across all dischargers—point and nonpoint—and a combined system of fees, permits, and central management offers multiple options for cost-effective control. The fact that a polluter can exit the association, or not join, imposes a constraint on the association's ability to raise price. The probability that the costs of monopoly control will exceed the gains from trade is reduced.

The position of the association is similar to that of a firm in a product market that may have superior technology and hence lower costs, the so-called dominant firm. Where entry and exit is not controlled, the dominant firm is expected to engage in entry-limit pricing, setting its price just below the marginal cost of any firm that might enter. The Tar-Pamlico authority faces a similar problem. A potential member can produce its own pollution control or purchase it from the association. If the association sets its fees too high, membership will decline. Entry and exit choices discipline the association manager.

The U.S. Environmental Protection Agency (1996) is currently pushing for the development of more river basin associations modeled after Tar-Pamlico. The agency explains its effort this way:

> Trading is an innovative way for water quality agencies and community stakeholders to develop common-sense, cost-effective solutions for water quality problems in their watersheds. . . . Trading can allow communities to grow and prosper while retaining their commitment to water quality. (U.S. Environmental Protection Agency 1996, xi)

Although the EPA announcement is something for market economists to celebrate, it is perplexing that it took more than twenty years for the initiative to arrive. At the time the EPA was formed, river basin associations were operating in the United States. These innovative water quality management systems were pushed to one side by command-and-control, technology-based regulation that has not been able to achieve the nation's water quality goals.[10]

WHAT ABOUT AIR POLLUTION?

A review of rights-based river basin associations tells us that common sense can influence outcomes and that command and control can be avoided. But what about air pollution? Can there be a counterpart to river basins? Perhaps. But to deal with the question, we must again focus on common-law rules.

History tells us that common law can protect air quality, and new technologies for satellite monitoring suggest that air-shed management is a clear possibility for protecting regional rights to air quality. For almost one hundred years, common-law courts protected air quality rights in the United States and Canada.[11] Recall that, at common law, no person has the right to impose cost on a neighbor against the neighbor's will. The law of nuisance and trespass protects the individual's property rights.

For decades, common-law judges heard air pollution cases brought by individuals and public defenders. When the damages befell a particular property owner, the owner went to court. When the harm affected a larger number of parties in a community or state, a public defender took up the case. Of course, common-law protection was never perfect, and common-law courts often attempted to balance benefits and costs, which works against property rights protection. But no single common-law court could impose rules on an entire nation. When errors were made, the effects fell on a few unlucky parties. Can we relate common-law remedies to air-shed management?

Satellite and other forms of pollution monitoring now make it possible for air pollution and its chemical components to be traced to major emission sources. Low-cost telecommunications can support continuous monitoring of emissions. In short, we have crossed a technology threshold that reduces the cost of transacting. The time is ripe to consider the combination of property rights, common law, and new technology for establishing air quality management for small and large regions.

To illustrate how the process might work, imagine an air-shed association or regional compact that defines air quality goals across the region. Private parties within the region can buy and sell the right to emit named pollutants (the terms of trade might differ depending on the locations of the trading parties). Continuous monitoring of emissions will assure that the seller of the rights has performed his part of the contract; the seller's emissions are reduced by the specified amount. Continuous monitoring also assures that the buyer has used no more emission rights than the amount purchased. Satellite monitoring focuses on the overall air quality for the air shed. If total emissions rise above the limits, action is taken by air-shed management to determine who is poaching on the system. Continuous monitoring can identify the culprit. Common-law suits would be brought against parties that violate the terms of the contracts or the rules of the association. The rule of law, market forces, and common-law courts would form the foundation for air pollution control.

As with the Tar-Pamlico River Basin Association, polluters would have an option. They could either join the air-shed management program or certify that they had installed the most restrictive form of pollution-control equipment. They could relocate to another air shed. Competition among air sheds would discipline monopoly tendencies of managers.

Is it possible to get from where we are today in air quality management to a system based on the rule of law? The policy distance is not as great as it first appears. The 1990 Clean Air Act made a sharp break with past statutes by giving clear recognition to the regional nature of the air pollution problem.[12] Yes, National Ambient Air Quality Standards remain in place and are tighter, but three specific regional problems were recognized: (1) The twenty-two cities that have not achieved the ozone standard, (2) California, which has peculiar nonattainment problems that are more severe than the rest of the nation's, and (3) a twelve-state ozone transport region, which includes the nation's northeastern quadrant. In each case, the statute turns to decentralized control. Although layered with bureaucratic concrete, the new rules require these regions to find innovative ways to address their air quality problems.

California has already developed an emissions trading market, where credits for emissions reductions are bought and sold (see Holden 1995; Passell 1995). Chicago has started another such market; other cities are experimenting with clean-fuel vehicles and community-based emissions controls. These emissions trades and community agreements are just one step away from the rules of common law. Indeed, the underlying contracts that accompany transfers will be enforced in common-law courts.

Contract enforcement relies on proof that reductions have occurred. Emissions monitoring is essential, and lower-cost monitoring and information management make it easier for the market to emerge. Property rights are emerging, and those rights must be protected. In every case, outcomes matter more than inputs. Command-and-control rules that focus on technologies are being replaced with performance standards.

One does not have to be a raging market optimist to envision a day when U.S. cities are given control of their environmental destiny. Rising incomes and new information about the value of the environmental envelope that sustains life deny the notion of a race to the bottom, where citizens will trade off the environment for the gains obtained from smokestack industries. With enough flexibility, market experiments will develop across the nation's metropolitan air sheds. Some will continue the costly and less-effective command and control of the past. Others will go with property rights and market forces. Still others will move to performance standards and third-party environmental audits. All will rely on continuous monitoring of emissions and contract enforcement. Citizens who prefer more environmental quality will vote with their feet. Local and state politicians will respond by searching for lower-cost ways to provide more-effective environmental protection. Eventually, the country will have the equivalent of environmental enterprise zones, where centralized control gives way to market forces, property rights, and more-effective environmental management.

Final Thoughts

The search in the United States for effective institutions to protect environmental rights has been costly but instructive. Early in the process, the nation chose to place environmental management in the hands of the federal government. Perhaps, at the time, that made sense, but what had been controlled by a rule of law and markets was subjected to the rule of politics. As a highly developed representative democracy, the new political economy responded in ways that are partly understood. Well-organized special-interest groups moved to Washington and participated in a new form of wealth redistribution that focused on command-and-control regulation. Constitutional rules that previously protected private property rights were stretched and in some cases broken. We have seen a regulatory state emerge, where major components of the nation's resource base are managed by monopoly regulators. The environmental saga has been costly. The high costs and growing global competition have induced a search for new technologies and lower-cost ways of monitoring outcomes. The information revolution has accommodated the search. Experiments have occurred under the heavy regulatory concrete. There is new learning that can be tapped. The world of the year 2000 is vastly different from the world of the 1970s, when the nation's environmental-control blueprint was first developed.

In considering a positive agenda for environmental policy that captures some of the changes now in the works, we should look for the following:[13]

- *Goal orientation.* Future environmental policy should place a premium on measuring, monitoring, and reporting on environmental quality. Progress toward specific goals, as set by communities, should be the measure of success, not the number of suits, enforcement actions, and installation of technology.

- *Flexibility.* Performance goals with complete flexibility for attaining them should be the general foundation for all environmental policy, with command and control occupying the default position. Innovation should be rewarded, not penalized. Valuable knowledge must be conserved.

- *Biological envelopes.* The environmental envelope that surrounds a community of environmental users should form the zone of control. River basin, watershed, and air-shed associations, as well as multistate compacts, should be encouraged and given flexibility in accomplishing goals. Again, the monitoring function is crucial.

- *Common sense.* Decision making for environmental protection should be located where outcomes and costs matter the most— at the level of the environmental user. People in communities can be trusted to protect themselves from harm. Those facing the problems have the greatest incentive to find the least-cost way of dealing with the problems. Local communities should rise to the top of the regulatory hierarchy.

- *Common law.* Steps should be taken to salvage common-law protection of private environmental rights. Statutory shields against common-law remedies should be eliminated, provided the community has participated in determining environmental goals and solutions.

- *Property rights.* Property rights should be respected. When private parties are asked to provide public benefits by altering the use of privately held rights, they should be paid.

Taken together, the above point toward communities, states, and regions and away from centralized control. Today environmental innovation areas are emerging; these form the wave of the future. National governments will have a heavy role to play in the continued search for environmental quality. But the role of central authorities will have more to do with setting standards for problems that are truly national in scope and monitoring outcomes than designing and fine-tuning the production processes of firms and industries nationwide.

As we consider elements for a new environmental policy, we do so recognizing that we live in a world that faces many other compelling demands, including health care, safety, retirement security, and education. Emerging communities elsewhere grapple with even more primitive wants and needs. Global competition is mentioned endlessly, and it is real.

In the struggle to secure environmental quality, we should seek the least-cost path, as measured by these other foregone opportunities. In my mind, that calls for flexibility in the face of scarcity. We seek to challenge our unlimited resources—the minds of men and women—to match the challenges that come from our more limited resources.

In prehistoric times, we are told, sharks and dinosaurs lived in the same periods. The dinosaur, full of bones and not very flexible, did not adjust and adapt. The shark, which does not have a bone in its body, only cartilage, made it to modern times. Our new environmental policy should be a shark, not a dinosaur.

Notes

1. For a discussion of costs and benefits, see Nelson (1993, 3).

2. A review of constitutional jurisprudence is found in O'Hara (1995).

3. For an interesting account of this and more, see Reinhardt (1993).

4. See Hahn and Hird (1991, 233–78). For discussion and comparison with other estimates, see U.S. Office of Management and Budget (1993, 4–5).

5. The discussion here is drawn from Probst et al. (1995).

6. For more on this, see Dalton (1993).

7. To varying degrees across the German states, the system of effluent charges has been in use for decades, some since 1904 (see Kneese and Bower 1984).

8. For most of the institutional story, see Riggs (1993), Sease (1993), Tar-Pamlico River Foundation, Inc. (1991), North Carolina (1989), and U.S. Environmental Protection Agency (1992).

9. The industrial firms and treatment works are referred to as point-source

dischargers, firms whose pollution discharge comes from a well-defined source or outfall. By contrast, the farmers are sources of nonpoint-source discharge, which may be generated when rain washes plowed fields as well as construction sites and city streets.

10. For a discussion of this earlier period, see Maloney and Yandle (1983).

11. For a review of the U.S. experience, see Meiners (1995). The Canadian experience is covered by Brubaker (1995).

12. For general background, see Tietenberg (1993, 450–75). See also Hahn (1993).

13. This is taken from Yandle (1996).

References

Bailey, Ronald. 1993. *Eco-Scam: The False Prophets of Ecological Apocalypse.* New York: St. Martin's Press.

Bast, Joseph L., Peter J. Hill, and Richard C. Rue. 1994. *Eco-Sanity.* Lanham, Md.: Madison Books.

Brubaker, Elizabeth. 1995. *Property Rights in the Defence of Nature.* London: Earthscan Publications.

Carson, Rachel. 1962. *Silent Spring.* Boston: Houghton-Mifflin Co.

Dalton, Brett A. 1993. "Superfund: The South Carolina Experience." In *Taking the Environment Seriously,* ed. Roger E. Meiners and Bruce Yandle. Lanham, Md.: Rowman and Littlefield Publishers.

Hahn, Robert W. 1989. "Economic Prescriptions for Environmental Problems." *Journal of Economic Perspectives* 3 (spring): 95–114.

———. 1993. "Choosing among Fuels and Technologies for Cleaning Up the Air." AEI Discussion Paper, American Enterprise Institute, Washington, D.C.

Hahn, Robert, and John Hird. 1991. "The Costs and Benefits of Regulation: Review and Synthesis." *Yale Journal of Regulation* 8 (winter): 233–78.

Holden, Benjamin A. 1995. "Dirt in Hollywood? Californians Have Pollution-Rights Market Ready for It." *Wall Street Journal,* April 12, p. B3.

Kneese, Alan V., and Blair T. Bower. 1984. *Managing Water Quality: Economics, Technology, Institutions.* Washington, D.C.: Resources for the Future.

Main, Jeremy. 1991. "The Big Cleanup Gets It Wrong." *Fortune,* May 20, 95–101.

Maloney, Michael T., and Bruce Yandle. 1983. "Building Markets for Tradable Pollution Rights." In *Water Rights,* ed. Terry L. Anderson. San Francisco: Pacific Institute for Public Policy Research.

Meiners, Roger E. 1995. "Elements of Property Rights: The Common Law Alternative." In *Land Rights: The 1990s' Property Rights Rebellion*, ed. Bruce Yandle. Lanham, Md.: Rowman and Littlefield Publishers.

Nelson, Robert H. 1993. "How Much Is Enough?" In *Taking the Environment Seriously*, ed. Roger E. Meiners and Bruce Yandle. Lanham, Md.: Rowman and Littlefield Publishers.

North Carolina. Division of Environmental Management. Water Quality Section. 1989. *Tar-Pamlico River Basin Nutrient Sensitive Waters Designation and Nutrient Management Strategy*. Raleigh, N.C.: Division of Environmental Management. Water Quality Section. April.

O'Hara, Erin. 1995. "Property Rights and the Police Power of the State: Regulatory Takings: An Oxymoron?" In *Land Rights: The 1990s' Property Rights Rebellion*, ed. Bruce Yandle. Lanham, Md.: Rowman and Littlefield Publishers.

Passell, Peter. 1995. "Illinois Is Looking to Market Forces to Help Reduce Its Smog." *New York Times*, March 30, p. C1.

Portney, Paul R. 1990a. "Air Pollution Policy." In *Public Policies for Environmental Protection*, ed. Paul R. Portney. Washington, D.C.: Resources for the Future.

———, ed. 1990b. *Public Policies for Environmental Protection*. Washington, D.C.: Resources for the Future.

Probst, Katherine N., Don Fullerton, Robert E. Litan, and Paul R. Portney. 1995. *Footing the Bill for Superfund Cleanup*. Washington, D.C.: Brookings Institution.

Reinhardt, Forest. 1993. *Du Pont Freon Products Division (A)*. Harvard Business School Case 9-389-111, Harvard Business School.

Riggs, David W. 1993. *Market Incentives for Water Quality: A Case Study of the Tar-Pamlico River Basin, North Carolina*. Clemson, S.C.: Center for Policy Studies, December.

Schneider, Keith. 1993. "A Policy That Set the World Standard Goes Off Track." *ECO*, June, pp. 17–22.

Sease, Les. 1993. "Overcoming Transaction Costs in Developing Markets for the Control of Nonpoint Source Pollution." Master's thesis, Department of Economics, Clemson University.

Tar-Pamlico River Foundation, Inc. 1991. *A River of Opportunity: A Pollution Abatement and Natural Resources Management Plan for the Pamlico Basin*. Washington, D.C.: Tar-Pamlico River Foundation, April.

Tietenberg, Tom. 1993. *Environmental and Natural Resource Economics*. New York: HarperCollins Publishers.

U.S. Environmental Protection Agency. 1987. *Unfinished Business*. Vol. 1: *Overview*. Washington, D.C.: U.S. Environmental Protection Agency, February.

———. 1992. *Managing Nonpoint Source Pollution*. Washington, D.C.: Office of Water and Office of Policy, Planning and Evaluation.

———. 1996. *Draft Framework for Watershed-Based Trading.* EPA 800-R-96-001. Washington, D.C.: U.S. Environmental Protection Agency, May.

U.S. Office of Management and Budget. 1993. *Regulatory Program of the United States Government, 1992–93.* Washington, D.C.: U.S. Government Printing Office.

Whelan, Elizabeth. 1985. *Toxic Terror.* Ottawa, Ill.: Jameson Books.

Yandle, Bruce. 1989. "Bootleggers and Baptists in the Market for Regulation." In *The Political Economy of Government Regulation,* ed. Jason F. Shogren. Boston: Kluwer Academic Publishers.

———. 1992. "Organic Constitutions and Common Law." *Constitutional Political Economy,* spring/summer, pp. 225–41.

———. 1996. *A Positive Agenda for Environmental Policy. The Shape of Things . . . ,* Essay no. 6. Washington, D.C.: Progress and Freedom Foundation, April.

Epilogue

It is possible to break the gridlock in environmental policy by using positive incentives. This means we must move beyond calls for mystical reverence for nature and toward policies that reward good stewardship. The first inhabitants of North America did this through private ownership of natural resources such as land, piñon forests, hunting territories, and salmon fishing streams. Following this tradition will help get the incentives right by turning environmental quality into an asset.

The following specific policy recommendations can be made politically palatable to voters across the political spectrum and can provide a starting point for breaking the environmental policy gridlock in Washington because they are based on common sense.

- Clearly specify the goals of ecosystem management as they relate to federal land and water managers so that those managers can be held accountable, in keeping with streamlining government and making it more effective.

- Allow long-term leasing of federal lands for purposes other than traditional commodity production. Specifically allow environmental organizations, for profit or not for profit, to lease federal lands for environmental amenities such as endangered species habitat.

- Follow the lead of school trust lands by earmarking net revenues from federal lands for specific uses so that the recipients of those funds will have an incentive to monitor and encourage improved efficiency in land management.

- Require federal land management agencies to cover costs out of user fees and designate any "profits" above costs for specific uses such as financing infrastructure in national parks, leasing private land for endangered species habitat, or financing Social Security deficits.

- Make permitted uses of federal lands, such as grazing permits, long term (e.g., ninety-nine years) and allow permit holders to transfer their permits to anyone including nonusers.

- Create a program wherein private landowners can bid to have their land leased by the government as endangered species habitat. Funding could come from recreational user fees on federal lands.

- Require compensation to landowners in all cases where property use is regulated to protect endangered species.

- Strictly follow the "polluter pays" principle but insist that federal agencies adhere to evidentiary rules before requiring a suspected polluter to pay.

- Require that all air and water quality regulations be specified in terms of performance standards rather than technology-based standards.

- Devolve authority for maintaining or improving air and water quality to states or even lower levels of government wherever the problems are confined to those jurisdictions.

Clearly there will be opposition to such reforms. Some environmentalists will argue that ecosystem management should be sufficiently vague to accommodate preservation agendas; that federal lands are theirs to use without charge; that private landowners have an obligation to provide endangered species habitat; or that all industrial waste should be reduced or eliminated regardless of demonstrated damage. On the other side, some producers will argue that leasing federal lands for environmental amenity production will destroy agricultural or logging communities; that endangered species should always take a backseat to jobs and the economy; or that technology-based standards are better because such standards can be manipulated to regulate competitors.

Despite these arguments, mustering a coalition for commonsense environmental reform should be feasible for political entrepreneurs. Win-win approaches relying on positive incentives reduce acrimony and allow environmental gains at less cost to the economy. Free market environmentalism is about two things: promoting economic growth that gives us the wealth, the technical capabilities, and the demand to promote environmental quality and using positive incentives to get environmental quality produced. Selling reforms that achieve these two goals, properly packaged, should not be difficult.

Contributors

Terry L. Anderson has been a professor of agricultural economics and economics at Montana State University since 1972 and is executive director of PERC, the Political Economy Research Center. Professor Anderson holds M.A. and Ph.D. degrees in economics from the University of Washington and a bachelor's degree from the University of Montana. Anderson has traveled and lectured extensively on six continents and been a visiting professor at renowned universities such as Stanford and Oxford. In addition to his teaching skills, which have won him several teaching awards, he is author or editor of fourteen books, including *Free Market Environmentalism*, which has been translated into three languages. He also has published numerous articles in professional journals and popular publications as diverse as the *Wall Street Journal* and *Fly Fisherman*. He is an avid outdoorsman who enjoys climbing frozen waterfalls and hunting with bow and arrow in Africa.

Ronald N. Johnson is a professor of economics at Montana State University in Bozeman, Montana. He received his Ph.D. in economics from the University of Washington in 1977. One of his main areas of concentration is natural resource economics. Johnson has published papers dealing with grazing, the auctioning of natural resources, water rights, the early conservation movement in the United States, fishery economics, log exports, and other forestry-related issues. An underlying theme in many of these papers is the analysis of property rights and the role these rights play in correcting environmental problems. His papers on resource economics have appeared in journals such as the *American Economic Review, Journal of Law & Economics, Economic Inquiry, American Journal of Agricultural Economics, Journal of Environmental Economics & Management, Southern Economic Journal, Journal of Economic History, Explorations in Economic History, Land Economics, Natural Resources Journal,* and *Marine Resource Economics.* Most recently, he has examined the introduction of individual transferable quotas in the New Zealand fishery and property issues in the forests of Honduras. In addition, he has coauthored seven articles and a book on the functioning of the federal bureaucracy. Johnson also participated in a recent national dialogue on ecosystem management, hosted by the Keystone Center.

DONALD R. LEAL, a senior associate at the Political Economy Research Center, has been carrying out research in natural resource and environmental issues since 1985. He received his B.S. in mathematics and M.S. in statistics from California State University at Hayward. He is a contributing author of *Multiple Conflicts over Multiple Uses* (1994), *Taking the Environment Seriously* (1993), and *The Yellowstone Primer: Land and Resource Management in the Greater Yellowstone Ecosystem* (1990). He is coauthor with Terry Anderson of *Free Market Environmentalism* (1991), which received the 1992 Choice Outstanding Academic Book Award, and is coauthor with Anderson of the forthcoming book *Enviro-Capitalists.* He has published numerous articles on such topics as fisheries, water, recreation, oil and gas, timber, and federal land use policy. His articles appear in newspapers such as the *Wall Street Journal, New York Times,* and *Chicago Tribune,* as well as specialized journals. Leal's recent studies comparing federal and state management of forests have fostered a new perspective on public land management.

RANDY T. SIMMONS is professor and department head of political science and director of the Institute of Political Economy at Utah State University. He received his Ph.D. in political science from the University of Oregon and has been a policy analyst in the Office of Policy Analysis at the U.S. Department of the Interior. He specializes in applying the assumptions and methods of economics to policy questions, especially to environmental and natural resource policy. His current research interest is in devolving national environmental policies to states, localities, and individuals. Simmons is coauthor with William Mitchell of *Beyond Politics: Bureaucracy, Welfare, and the Failure of Bureacracy.*

RICHARD L. STROUP is a professor of economics at Montana State University and a senior associate of PERC (the Political Economy Research Center) in Bozeman, Montana. He was born in Sunnyside, Washington, in 1943 and received his B.A., M.A., and Ph.D. from the University of Washington. From 1982 to 1984, he was director of the Office of Policy Analysis at the U.S. Department of the Interior. For a more complete biography, see *Who's Who in America.*

Stroup is a widely published author and speaker on economics, including natural resources and environmental issues. He has also written on public choice, tax policy, and labor economics. His work has been a major force in the development of the approach to resource problems known as the new resource economics, or free-market environmentalism. He is coauthor, with James D. Gwartney, of a recent primer on economics, *What Everybody Should Know about Economics and Prosperity,* and of a leading economics principles textbook, *Economics: Private and Public Choice* (Dryden, 1995), now in its seventh edition, as well as *Introduction to Economics: The Wealth and Poverty of Nations* (Dryden, 1994).

Other books include *National Resources: Bureaucratic Myths and Environmental Management* (Ballinger, 1983), written with John Baden, and *Bureaucracy vs. the Environment: The Environmental Cost of Bureaucratic Governance* (University of Michigan Press, 1981), edited with John Baden. He has also written many articles for professional journals and for popular media outlets. His most recent research has focused on alternative institutional arrangements for dealing with endangered species, regulatory takings, hazardous waste, and other environmental risks.

Stroup is a Cato adjunct scholar and a member of the Mont Pelerin Society.

BRUCE YANDLE is Alumni Distinguished Professor of Economics and Legal Studies at Clemson University, where he has been a faculty member since 1969, and a senior associate with the Political Economy Research Center. He has served in Washington on two occasions. In 1976–1978, he was a senior economist on the White House staff, where he reviewed and analyzed newly proposed environmental regulations. In 1982–1984, he was executive director of the Federal Trade Commission. He serves on the advisory boards of the Environmental Issues Council and the International Center for Environmental Policy Research in Paris. He is a member of the South Carolina State Board of Economic Advisers.

Yandle's research and teaching focus on government regulation and policy. He is author/editor of eleven books including *Environmental Use and the Market, The Political Limits of Environmental Regulation, Regulatory Reform in the Reagan Era, Taking the Environment Seriously,* and *Land Rights: The 1990s' Property Rights Rebellion.*

Before entering a career in university teaching and research, Yandle was in the industrial machinery business for fifteen years. A native of Georgia, he received his A.B. degree from Mercer University and his MBA and his Ph.D. degrees from Georgia State University.

Index